BEYOND the MIRROR

Seeing YOURSELF THE WAY GOD SEES YOU

Ta'Tyana Leonard

BEYOND the MIRROR

Seeing YOURSELF THE WAY GOD SEES YOU

Ta'Tyana Leonard

ISION STATEMENT

Restoring Vision... Identity...Purpose
Los Angeles, California

To my nieces
Uriah, Rebecka, Arrington, Cairo, and NyAirra

I praise you because I am fearfully and wonderfully made;
your works are wonderful, I know that full well.
Psalm 139:14

Contents

Introduction

I carry a burden, a heavy load, which leaves me heartbroken and concerned for women around the world. Women of all ages and seasons of life can find themselves in a desperate place, a place where we do not know who we are; a place where we do not know our purpose or where we do not believe in ourselves. This place leads us to search for answers and ways to fix ourselves. Where we search for these answers will determine how we live the rest of lives. Where we search for these answers concerns my heart to its very core.

Where we search is my burden. I've witnessed so many women search to answer questions of purpose, identity, and self-worth in all the wrong places. Relationships, careers, money, success, and even failures will not lead us to the answers. So, this burden led me to write. My burden to help women find their purpose and identity in the right place propelled me to write *Beyond the Mirror: Seeing Yourself the Way God Sees You.*

The Root

While serving with Fellowship of Christian Athletes as a campus Minister to South Los Angeles public high schools, I recognized a dark reality. This dark reality left mere teenagers to live in the brokenness of depression, prom-iscuity, sex trade, sexuality, and abortion. At such a young age these women were carrying heavy loads of shame and guilt. As I got to know their stories, God helped me to identify a common root of their brokenness: self- worth!

These young women did not know their true worth and had settled for discounts. We are not any different from these girls. We all allow the world's standards to impact how we view ourselves. But here's the problem: How we view ourselves, affects our entire lives. Knowing our value and purpose is crucial because our self-worth affects decision-making and interaction with the world around us. Our per-ceived self -worth affects how we see others, how we face trials, and ultimately determines our success in life. This is why God wants us to seek our true worth in Him, not in the standards of the world.

I've learned too often that the world's standards on beauty and success is completely opposite of what God says. Today, our society uses bank accounts and twitter followers to determine one's value, while God looks at the heart. *People look at the outward appearance, but the Lord looks at the heart* (1 Samuel 16:7).

Beyond the Mirror was written to help you see your-self the way your Heavenly Father sees you. After all, it's His opinion of you that matters most. So grab your Bible and jour-nal as we take a journey centered in truth; a journey that will help us to see ourselves the way God sees us!

Seeing in "God Vision"

How do we see others, and ourselves, the way God sees us? How can we look past the exterior to see the heart? Well, we must see the world and ourselves through "God Vi-sion." God can renew our minds and hearts to see the world from His perspective. Let's take a look at how God shook up the prophet Samuel and his perception of what the future King of Israel should look like.

Israel was in need of a new king. Samuel, a priest and prophet of the Lord, was sent to the home of Jesse to select a king from among Jesse's sons. When Samuel reached the home of Jesse, he first meets Eliab, one of Jesse's older sons, strong in stature. Because of Eliab's appearance, Samuel thought surely the chosen future King stood before him. However, God quickly shuts down Samuel's simple thinking. God responds:

Do not consider his appearance or his height, for I have rejected him. The Lord does not look at the things people look at. People look at the outward appearance, but the Lord looks at the heart (1 Samuel 16:7).

Israel's first king, Saul, was chosen based on his physical attributes. The Bible notes, *there was no one more impressive among the Israelites. Saul stood a head taller than anyone else* (1 Samuel 9.2). Having based his perceptions on how Israel's king had been chosen in the past, Samuel was commanded by God to reject this old way of thinking. God's plan for choosing a new king was to go deeper than just physical stature.

Read 1 Samuel 16: 7-13 (NIV)

But the Lord said to Samuel, "Do not consider his appearance or his height, for I have rejected him. The Lord does not look at the things people look at. People look at the outward appearance, but the Lord looks at the heart."

Then Jesse called Abinadab and had him pass in front of Samuel. But Samuel said, "The Lord has not chosen this one either." Jesse then had Shammah pass by, but Samuel said, "Nor has the Lord chosen this one." Jesse had seven of his sons pass before Samuel, but Samuel said to him, "The Lord has not chosen these." So he asked Jesse, "Are these all the sons you have?"

"There is still the youngest," Jesse answered. "He is tending the sheep." Samuel said, "Send for him; we will not sit down until he arrives."

So he sent for him and had him brought in. He was glowing with health and had a fine appearance and handsome features. Then the Lord said, "Rise and anoint him; this is the one."

So Samuel took the horn of oil and anointed him in the presence of his brothers, and from that day on the Spirit of the Lord came powerfully upon David. Samuel then went to Ramah.

Learning From David

What can we learn from David? David was a young man; scholars believe he was between 10-14 years old when he was anointed by Samuel to become Israel's new king. David's age and stature caused many to believe he lacked maturity, wisdom, and strength, and was not suitable to be a king. Despite the realities of David's experience and age, God used David in a mighty way. Overtime, as he trusted in God, he became an ideal king.

- David was known as a great warrior who killed the giant Philistine Goliath.
- David reigned over Israel for 40 years
- David wrote half of the Book of Psalms
- David is praised in the Book of Hebrews 11 as a "Hero of Faith"

God looked beyond David's lack of credentials and made him into a mighty king. David was not a perfect king; however with God's help, he founded a dynasty. Will you learn from David's story and allow God to make you great? Can you look beyond your current circumstances and see the great future God has in store for you?

On this journey to seeing yourself the way God sees you, we will explore the Bible to learn how and why we were created, realize the freedom we have to succeed, and accept the calling to live in our purpose.

How to Use *Beyond the Mirror*?

This book is designed to help women find their true identity and worth in Jesus Christ. The goal of *Beyond the Mirror* is to teach biblical truths of how and why we were created, in order to steer women in the direction of their true purpose and calling. When women see themselves the way God sees them, their potential is limitless. The problem is many women do not know where to start to find their identity and purpose. *Beyond the Mirror* provides tools and exercises for personal study and application, intending to lead women into the life they were created to live.

Each chapter has three parts: Biblical Examination, Reflection Questions, and Spiritual Disciplines. *Biblical Examination* consists of Scripture and commentary to further explain the Holy text. We will examine the original languages (Hebrew and Greek) of the Bible to find fuller meaning and background of Scripture. *Biblical Examination* will be followed by *Reflection Questions* to make the Scripture personal. *Reflection Questions* will lead to a richer understanding of the text, but will also place you within the biblical text to experience the hand of God. Finally each chapter concludes with a Spiritual Discipline.

Spiritual Discipline

Spiritual Disciplines are exercises or activities that open us to God. They are called disciplines because they start with a disciplined effort to do something new. Spiritual Disciplines take us out of our normal routines and leave us open to let God use us. The new action moves us into a healthy spiritual habit that strengthens our faith. Each chapter will conclude with a *Spiritual Discipline in Action*, and all readers are encouraged to focus on that discipline for an entire week. As you learn more about the various disciplines and begin to practice each one weekly, try to incorporate your favorites into your daily routine.

Keep a Journal

Beyond the Mirror allots room for reflection question answers and notes; however, readers are encouraged to keep a journal while reading this book. Journaling allows us to make note of what is being revealed to us on this journey. Journaling also allows us to write and reflect in the moment. While on this journey, you do not want to miss or forget anything God may be placing on your heart.

Pray

Finally, ask God to open your heart and mind to what you read. *For such a time as this*, God has placed this book in your hands. Pray to start this book with a spirit of openness, of understanding, and completion. Pray for God to give you a desire to go deeper and the dedication to take the time to read weekly. Then ask God to give you wisdom and awareness of the message He has specifically for you.

The Power of Community

Think about the most transformative moments of your life. Good or bad, who was around? Who had influence in your life choices? Who supported your decisions? Who cheered you on? Who discouraged you? The people around you in these moments helped to shape your social setting. These moments prove the power of our community and social settings. And these people may have also had more influence on your decisions than you want to admit.

Humans are created for community and relationship—for a relationship with God and with others. This is why Jesus states the most important command is to *Love the Lord your God with all your heart and with all your soul and with all your strength and with all your mind; and, Love your neighbor as yourself* (Luke 10:27).

Dallas Willard notes how transformation is profoundly social. "For all that is between me and God affects who I am; and that, in turn, modifies my relationship to everyone around. My relationship to others also modifies me and deeply affects my relationship to God. Hence those relationships must be transformed if I am to be transformed."[1]

In others words, if we want change, our community must also change. Many of us attempt to tackle change in isolation. However, we were created in the image of a Triune God (Father, Son, And Holy Spirit), who dwells in eternal community. Made in the likeness of God, we are community dwellers, and any form of change will be more impactful in the presence of others.

The best way to enter into the *Beyond the Mirror* journey is with others. Community provides accountability, confirmation, and encouragement. Please invite others along for the journey. Trust me, road trips are so much more fun with your girls along for the ride!

What do you see?

CHAPTER 1

How You Were Created

*I praise you because I am fearfully and wonderfully
made; your works are wonderful, I know that full well*
(Psalm 139:14).

The first step in seeing yourself the way God sees you is learning how you were created. How one is created lends not only to one's worth, but also to what one is purposed for. In general, items are created to fulfill a need or to enhance life. Consumer demands combined with the quality of a product determines its value. For example, let's take a look at a popular household item, the "cast iron skillet." The cast iron skillet is renowned for its ability to retain and defuse heat. Cast iron skillets are produced from a single piece of metal so they have the ability to distribute heat evenly. The secret to the production of a quality skillet is the mineral levels in the "iron recipe." Irons with high carbon content are added to powered chemicals to agglomerate the natural impurities in the iron and heated to 1500°C. The iron is then pressed into a two-part mold to produce the cookware's shape.

Now that you are an expert on how cast iron skillets are made, it's clear that these skillets were made for a particular purpose. The process in which these skillets are made allows them to serve a dual-purpose as stovetop fryers or an oven, baking dish. The cast iron skillets' ability to withstand excessive heat sets it apart from other types of pots and pans which would get damaged at temperatures of 400°F or more.

The cast iron skillet's unique production process makes it multi-functional, and a mainstay in any kitchen. If the manner in which cookware is made defines its worth and purpose; the process in which you were created must tell something about you as well. Let's take a look at the process of God's creation of all living things.

The Creation Story
In the beginning God created the heavens and the earth
(Genesis 1:1).

The first book of the Bible, Genesis, which means *origin* or *beginning,* proves God is our creator and created all living things. God first lays the groundwork for humans to inhabit and possess the earth. God lays the foundation of light, land, sea, vegetation, and animals to provide for Adam, the first man. God's creative process gives important insight to God's purpose for His creation.

When it came to mankind, God had a plan to create a being that reflected His image and likeness. Both male and female were created in the great image of God.

So God created mankind in his own image, in the image of God he created them; male and female he created them (Genesis 1:27).

The Image of God

What is the image and likeness of God? How is the image and likeness of God revealed in creation? These are questions we will answer in this chapter. The Creation Story reveals the process of God's creative work. The process in which God creates reveals a unique plan for each created being. Before we take a look at how the created reflects the Creator, let's take a look at the character of God. The Bible clearly depicts the character of God; here are a few attributes of God noted in Scripture:

Love—God is love and is the only pure and complete definition of love. God loves His creation and the Bible teaches nothing can separate us from His love. Nothing we can do will make God love us any less. God demonstrates His love through forgiveness and sacrifice, even to the point of death.

For God so loved the world that he gave his one and only Son, that whoever believes in him shall not perish but have eternal life (John 3:16).

Sovereign—God is sovereign and autonomous. He is an excellent ruler that reigns with matchless power and authority. All things are under His feet and all things are under His control.

Jesus looked at them and said, "With man this is impossible, but with God all things are possible" (Matthew 19:26).

Holy—God is good, holy, and righteous. He defines and sets the standard for what is good and pure.

But just as He (God) who called you is holy, so be holy in all you do (1 Peter 1:15).

Wise—God is the source of all true wisdom and knowledge. He informs the world of what is real and true. His wise plan formed the foundations of the heavens and the earth.

By wisdom the Lord laid the earth's foundations, by understanding he set the heavens in place (Proverbs 3:19).

True—God is truth and all truth comes from Him. God's reality is the only true perspective. God is trustworthy: true to His word and to His promises.

> *Now this is eternal life: that they know you, the only true God, and Jesus Christ, whom you have sent (John 17:3).*

Unchangeable—God is who He is. God is a constant divine being that remains unchanged by the world and circumstances.

> *Jesus Christ is the same yesterday and today and forever (Hebrews 13:8).*

God intentionally chose to form both male and female in His image and likeness. "The 'image' is man's indelible constitution as a rational and morally responsible being, and the 'likeness' is that spiritual accord with the will of God."[2] God chose mankind to be a representative figure of His power, intellect, and love upon the earth. The list above depicts the greatness of God; the list above also describes the very essence you were created to reflect to the world. Doesn't this make you want to experience more of what God has created you for?

Reflection Questions
1. What is the difference between the image and likeness of God?

2. How does it feel to learn that you were created to be a "representative" of God on earth?

Representative

I was an athlete throughout grade school and college. I took pride in representing something larger than myself. I felt responsible to represent my team, organization, or school with respect and dignity. I knew my actions would impact not just me, but my team. At times I felt pressure to represent my team well, but the pressure also pushed me to live with character. I was pushed to make honorable decisions, even when I thought no one was watching.

Similarly to representing a team, we represent our Creator. We were created for the purpose of reflecting and showing the world who created us. We represent something larger than ourselves. We represent God.

Wow, what pressure? No, let's change that to . . . what an honor! We are graced with the honor to represent God. We were created specifically to represent God, and bear His image. Let's continue to take a look at how God's methods in creation lend to our worth and purpose.

The Progression of Artistry
God saw all that he had made, and it was very good
(Genesis 1:31).

No other creation had the privilege of being created in the image of the Creator God. To create mankind as a representative required a progression in artistry. A progression means things continued to get better; God's creation began to have a heightened function and purpose. Although God looked upon all of His creation and saw that *it was very good*, humans were at the height of God's creative work. Genesis notes God "created" the earth and animals, but He "formed" mankind. The word *formed* in the original Old Testament Hebrew language is *yatsar (yaw-tsar')*, which means to mold into a form, especially as a potter; or to purpose. This heightened work of art proves the difference in responsibility and purpose above any other being. Read and compare God's purpose for creatures and mankind:

Creatures - Genesis 1:22

> *God blessed them and said, "Be fruitful and increase in number and fill the water in the seas, and let the birds increase on the earth."*

Mankind- Genesis 1:28

> *God blessed them and said to them, "Be fruitful and increase in number; fill the earth and subdue it. Rule over the fish in the sea and the birds in the sky and over every living creature that moves on the ground."*

The two verses above are referred to as the *blessings* given to God's creation. They are called *blessings* instead of *commands* because through them, God reveals His purpose and cause for existence. By the very Word of the Creator, mankind is the beneficiary of God's land and is also commissioned to display His authority on earth. Being created in the image of God, authority is presumed to mankind's nature, showing God's intention to make mankind a ruling force on earth as He rules in Heaven.

The Formation of the Woman

Moses, the author of Genesis, briefly depicts the formation of mankind in Chapter One, but goes in depth with the creation of man and woman in Chapter Two. Moses depicts how God formed Adam from the dust of the ground and breathed the breath of life into his nostrils. As the land began to produce fruit, God planted a garden in a place called Eden, which means *paradise*. Adam was given few instructions: work and watch over the land and eat freely from any tree, except from the tree of *the knowledge of good and evil.*

With a short list of duties, Adam worked the land but found no companion like himself. So God knowing *It is not good for the man to be alone* (Genesis 2:18) made Adam a suitable helper.

> *Then the Lord God made a woman from the rib he had taken out of the man, and he brought her to the man. The man said,*
> *"This one, at last, is now bone of my bones*
> *and flesh of my flesh;*
> *she shall be called 'woman,'*
> *for she was taken out of man"*
> *(Genesis 2:22-23 HCSB).*

The Unique Creation: Woman

"At last," Adam exclaims with joy and wonder as he awakes from his slumber. He viewed God's most beautiful creation. Adam took pride in knowing that God's most beautiful creation was formed from parts of his own body. He undoubtedly thought, "Wow she came from me!" Adam named her *woman, for she was taken out of man.* Adam later named her Eve, which means *life giver.* Adam's response to Eve proves she was a sight to see. However, the original Hebrew language provides a richer illustration of how the woman was truly formed by God.

Throughout the story of creation we learn that God "created" the heavens, earth, and animals; but "formed" mankind in His own image and likeness. When it comes to the formation of Eve, the Hebrew word used is *banah (bawnaw'),* and it is distinct from any other words used to depict the creation process. The word *banah* means built or fashioned. Many Bible scholars believe the word *fashioned* means Eve was constructed and skillfully formed by the hands of God. Other occurrences of the word *banah* throughout the Old Testament are used for the construction of palaces, temples, and altars, which means the woman was God's first aesthetic work. In other words, you are God's masterpiece.

"Wow-Man" is Adam's response to Eve. Her beauty exceeded all of God's created work. The word *banah* proves women are God's greatest aesthetic work. God's progression in artistry, meaning things continued to get better, ended with us! Even without makeup and manicures, we represent the beauty of God. This responsibility, like any other duty or charge, can lead to pressure. Women feel an immense pressure to meet the beauty standards of our culture.

Where did this pressure begin? How did the gift of beauty become a curse? How did beauty become a measure of a woman's worth? Why do we accept pressure, which God does not project upon us? In short, this pressure began in the Garden of Eden. We will later learn how sin has corrupted our ability to see ourselves the way God sees us. However, the Bible simply says we are beautiful, we are God's masterpieces, and that settles it.

How God Created the Woman

How we were created lends to how God cared for and purposed His creation. Created in the image of God, we learned mankind was to reflect His likeness on earth, through reigning over the land and displaying God's authority on earth. The woman was also formed to be a representative of God on earth alongside Adam. Together they were to procreate, and co-rule the land. The relationship between man and woman is conveyed through the term *ezer kənegdōw (ê-zer kə-neḡ-dōw)*, which means "suitable helper." The term *helper* is not a term of inferiority, but signifies purpose and mutuality.

Adam's fruitless search for a companion and helpmate opened his eyes to how God created him differently from other living creatures. No other creature could match Adam's intellect, reasoning, and spirit, for mankind was created for a superior function and purpose.

It is important to note that God didn't create Eve until Adam realized a need for her. Adam knew Eve's true worth. Adam needed Eve. Eve was created to fulfill a need through companionship and to enhance life through co-rulership. God was pleased with His creation of mankind. He ordained Adam and Eve to reflect, relate, and reign on earth: *Reflect* the image and likeness of God, *relate* as one as God is one, and *reign* over the earth. In the chapters to come, we will learn what it means to *reflect*, *relate*, and *reign*.

Spiritual Discipline in Action

Discipline—*Praying Scripture*

Purpose: To allow God to shape, form, and influence your prayers through the written Word of God. This opens the heart to God's truth through psalms, hymns, promises, prayers, and testimonies found in Scriptures. Prayer is simply talking to God. Through prayer we can express our feelings, attitudes, and requests to God. Praying Scripture allows us to speak the truth of God's Word over our life and positions us to pray the will of God.

Words Are Important

Words are important to God. God created the heavens, earth, and mankind with His very words. Being created in the image and likeness of God, we possess similar authority and creative power with our words. From a young age I learned the power of words. For years I was crippled by the fear of rejection by words uttered to me on the playground: *You're stupid.* Those words hurt severely. I struggled in grade school and always felt an immense pressure to prove my intelligence. This pressure crept its way into my health (I suffered from stress related digestive disorders), self-esteem, relationships, and what I felt worthy to receive.

Later I learned the root of my ambition and even unnecessary busyness was to prove that I wasn't stupid. The words we speak to others and over our own lives effect how we live and see ourselves. The spiritual discipline of *praying scripture* will help transform our language into God language. Here are a few verses that helped me grow closer to seeing myself the way God sees me.

Take 20 minutes to pray and reflect upon the following Scriptures. Allow God to guide your prayer through praying the following verses over your life and making it personal. Insert your name and claim the promises of God.

I praise you because I am fearfully and wonderfully made; your works are wonderful, I know that full well (Psalm 139:14).

For we are God's masterpiece. He has created us anew in Christ Jesus, so we can do the good things he planned for us long ago (Ephesians 2:10 NLT).

Tips: Praise God for how He created you and make the Scripture personal. Pray about the source of confidence these Scriptures give you. Pray about the possible "good things" God has created you specifically to do.

Chapter Overview

1. How one is created lends not only to one's worth, but also to what one is purposed for.

2. Both male and female were created in the great image of God.

3. God elected mankind to be a representative figure of His power, intellect, and love upon the earth.

4. Being created in the image of God, authority is presumed to mankind's nature; showing God's intention to make mankind a ruling force on earth as He is in Heaven.

5. The word *banah* means built or fashioned. Many Bible scholars believe that the word *fashioned* means that Eve was constructed and skillfully formed by the hands of God.

6. The relationship between man and woman is conveyed through the term *'ê-zer kə-neḡ-dōw* which means *suitable helper*. The term *helper* is not a term of inferiority, but signifies purpose and mutuality.

7. God was pleased with His creation of mankind and ordained them to reflect, relate, and reign: Reflect the image and likeness of God, Relate as one as God is one, and Reign over the earth.

Related Scriptures:

- Psalm 119:3
- Psalm 139:13-16
- Isaiah 64:8
- 2 Corinthians 3:1

CHAPTER 2

Why You Were Created

For we are God's masterpiece. He has created us anew in Christ Jesus, so we can do the good things he planned for us long ago (Ephesians 2:10 NLT).

C an you imagine receiving an unexpected inheritance, an inheritance that made you an heir to fortunes? What would you buy first? How would you use this power? I don't know about you, but I have a list of things I would do with this newfound fortune. The sky is the limit, and there seems to be so much freedom in financial security. When I dream without fear or financial restrictions, I dream big! When I dream about the "good works" God has created me to accomplish, I think big—like super bowl big! However, my dreams aren't currently my reality.

What if we all lived with a "dream big" mindset? What if we lived without fear or restriction? Trust me, my life is a daily exchange of faith over fear. I settle, I quit, and I run away when I feel incapable. However, I am growing in faith every day and trusting God will provide all I need to accomplish His plans for my life. Even stepping out in faith to write this book is a growth experience. I thought: "Who wants to listen to me?" "I don't have enough credentials, and I am not a well-known name." However, the Lord has given me a word to share with His daughters, and I am acting in obedience to share these words with you. As I write, I am trusting God will provide ways to get this book into the hands of women. I am trusting that my obedience to write will result in lives being changed.

So, let's get back to the question. What if I told you that you are actually an heir to a lavish inheritance? Would you believe me? Well, believe it or not, you are the recipient of the most lavish inheritance. You are an "Heiress!" We are the beneficiary of God's image and likeness, which makes us His *Image Bearers*. These blessings are an inheritance given from God the Father to His children. This inheritance is greater than any financial gain we can ever receive. This inheritance confirms our purpose. And as we grasp being formed in the image of God, we see how we innately preserve heavenly blessings as *Image Bearers.*

Answering the question of why you were created confirms your purpose. We are heirs to God's Image; this is why we were created. We will take a closer look at our inheritance in the following chapters, but for now we will learn how God equips us to successfully bear and reflect His image.

Heiress

Today, when people think of an heiress many may think of Paris Hilton. Paris, the great granddaughter of Hilton Hotel's founder, Conrad Hilton, has become the modern day prototype of an heiress, and unfortunately she is also the most infamous. Paris has coined the term *heiress* and because of her fame, many associate heirs with instant fame, Reality TV, party life, and sex tapes. Today's understanding of an inheritance centers on the person receiving the fortune: What did they do to deserve it? How will they make a name for themselves? Will they bring honor or disgrace to the family name? However, a true inheritance actually has nothing to do with the person receiving the inheritance; but centers on the giver. It is the benefactor's success and riches that are being passed on; it is their legacy that's at stake. As beneficiaries of God's irrevocable blessings, we have great responsibility to keep our inheritance *God Centered.* We must be about our Father's business.

An inheritance in the legal sense refers to a transfer of property after the death of a family member. The Bible renews the idea of inheritance to include the acquisition of promises and spiritual blessings from God. God is our benefactor and chooses to bestow material and spiritual blessings to mankind. In the Old Testament Scripture, the word *blessing* is *bārak (baw-rak')*, which means kneel; bless; to bestow power for success. In the English text, we may overlook "blessings" as just another gift from God. However, when God blessed mankind He blessed us with the power to be successful in our purpose. We must trust that God blesses His creation with all we need to successfully fulfill our purpose as His *Image Bearers.*

Reflection Questions
1. How does it feel to learn that you are an *heiress*?

2. You were created to be an heir, to handle the business of your Heavenly Father. Does this responsibility inspire you or frighten you? And why?

3. The Hebrew word for *blessing* is: *bārak (baw-rak')*, which means kneel; bless; to bestow power for success. In what ways do you feel God has "bestowed power" upon you for "success"?

Blessed for Success

God has bestowed upon you the power for success, to accomplish your purpose as His *Image Bearer*. Some may still believe they are incapable or inadequate to be a rightful heir of God's image. However, the Bible constantly gives examples of God using those who appear inadequate to accomplish His will. Let's take a look at a humble village girl, who was called a peasant in many circles because she lived in poverty in a town called Nazareth. She was from an insignificant town that many looked down upon. And to add to her lowly situation, she was 14 years old and an unwed mother.

Despite her circumstances, this young lady became one of the most well known women in the world. She became known for her faith and character. And today continues to hold the highest honors amongst mothers. She was wed to a carpenter, and together they raised her first born, who became a teacher and healer. Her son eventually became a mighty King and a Savior to the World.

Who is this woman of faith? Who is this success story? This woman would be Mary, the Mother of Jesus. Among all the godly Jewish women of that time, Mary was the chosen vessel God used to mother Jesus, the Savior of the World and the Son of God. God used a humble town, Nazareth, and a lowly servant to rear His Son.

So let's set the scene. Mary was a virgin preparing to marry her fiancé Joseph. But there was a problem: she was a virgin and pregnant. Joseph and Mary had not been intimate, and her pregnancy brought tension and doubt into their relationship. Who would believe Mary was still a virgin when she clearly showed signs of being pregnant? Can you imagine how Joseph felt? As a result of Mary's pregnancy, Joseph planned to divorce Mary. Mary would face social humiliation from an illegitimate pregnancy and a divorce. Yet Mary is surprisingly willing to submit to the will of God and trust Him even in the confusion of the situation. Let's take a look at her encounter with the Angel Gabriel:

Luke 1: 26b-33

> *God sent the angel Gabriel to Nazareth, a town in Galilee, to a virgin pledged to be married to a man named Joseph, a descendant of David. The virgin's name was Mary. The angel went to her and said, "Greetings, you who are highly favored! The Lord is with you." Mary was greatly troubled at his words and wondered what kind of greeting this might be. But the angel said to her, "Do not be afraid, Mary; you have found favor with God. You will conceive and give birth to a son, and you are to call him Jesus. He will be great and will be called the Son of the Most High. The Lord God will give him the throne of his father David, and he will reign over Jacob's descendants forever; his kingdom will never end."*

Although Mary was troubled by her encounter with the Angel, Mary built up enough courage to ask the angel, "*How can this be since I am a virgin.*" Gabriel explained how the Holy Spirit would come upon her and allow her to become pregnant. This would be a baby conceived of the Holy Spirit, *so the holy one to be born will be called the Son of God* (Luke 1:33).

Mary's Response
"I am the Lord's servant," Mary answered. "May your word to me be fulfilled"(Luke 1:38 NIV).

Mary was a teenager, unmarried, and an inexperienced mother. She could have presented Gabriel with excuses and a list of reasons why she was not capable of rearing the Savior of the world. However, Mary made no excuses and committed herself as a *servant* of the Lord. In the original Greek text the word *servant* is *doulé (doo'-lay),* which means a slave, or bondman, or metaphorically, one who gives himself up wholly to another's will. Mary was invited to become part of the divine plan of Salvation and despite not having all the answers, gave herself fully to the will of God.

Reflection Questions

1. Mary was only a teenager when God invited her to mother the Son of God. How would you have reacted if you were in her position?

2. Mary was a teenager facing social humiliation, but was willing to give herself wholly to the will of God. Mary was willing to trust God even when she didn't have all of the answers. What might be holding you back from giving yourself wholly to the will of God?

God's Response

Mary surrendered her will and body to the divine plan of the Lord. Mary agreed to allow God to use her as an instrument of hope, so that through her, a Savior would be born. Mary responded in faith and her obedience resulted in God's provision. The events in Mary's life after she accepted the invitation to mother the Savior of the world were evidence that God would direct paths and provide all we would need to fulfill His purpose. Let's take a closer look at God's provision in Mary's life.

Provision Through Joseph

Mary was betrothed to Joseph and planned to marry the following year. The Jewish marriage customs of the time occurred in 3 stages. First the engagement, which is often arranged by a marriage broker when two people are children. Second, the betrothal, which is a one-year period where the couple is considered "married" but do not have sexual relations. The third stage was the official marriage. Mary and Joseph were in the second, the betrothal stage, and had not been intimate. The engagement and betrothal were actual legal contracts and called for a divorce to officially end the relationship.

Joseph's character is defined by how he receives the news of Mary's pregnancy. Since Joseph was not the father of Mary's child, he assumed that Mary had committed adultery. Despite the news of Mary's pregnancy, Joseph is gentle in spirit and does not want to disgrace her publicly. He decides to divorce her secretly, which would avoid public shame and even public punishment. The Old Testament punishment for adultery was the stoning of both guilty parties to death (Deuteronomy 22:23-24). Joseph, being a righteous man, prepared to do what he thought was best to protect Mary. God, knowing the thoughts of Joseph, sent an angel to step in and inform Joseph of what was really going on:

But after he had considered this, an angel of the Lord appeared to him in a dream and said, "Joseph son of David, do not be afraid to take Mary home as your wife, because what is conceived in her is from the Holy Spirit. She will give birth to a son, and you are to give him the

*name Jesus, because he will save his people from their
sins."*

*All this took place to fulfill what the Lord had said
through the prophet: "The virgin will conceive and give
birth to a son, and they will call him Immanuel," which
means "God with us" (Matthew 1: 20-23).*

When Joseph awoke from his dream, he obeyed all
the angel instructed him to do. Joseph was wed to Mary soon
after and was not intimate with her until she gave birth to Jesus. God provided Mary with a husband to walk alongside her
on this divine path. Joseph, as a husband, provided companionship, financial provision, and physical protection, ultimately legitimizing Mary's extraordinary circumstance to an
on-looking world.

Provision Through Elizabeth

Scriptures note Mary's knowledge of the Old Testament prophesies of a coming Savior, for the angel Gabriel exclaims, *"The Lord is with you,"* emphasizing her character and
faith. God knew Mary's heart. He knew she would respond
in faith. But God also knew her situation would be better if
He provided a companion who understood the blessings of a
miraculous birth. When the angel Gabriel explained Mary's
role in God's salvation plan, he shared that her relative Elizabeth was also pregnant. Elizabeth's pregnancy was significant to Mary because Elizabeth was barren and was well
beyond her child-bearing years. Although Elizabeth and her
husband Zechariah were a righteous couple and living without blame, Elizabeth's barrenness was looked down upon.
This too shows God's provision and purpose.

Gabriel told Mary to *consider your relative Elizabeth, even she has conceived a son in her old age, and this is
the sixth month for her who was called childless. For nothing
will be impossible with God* (Luke 1:36-37 HCSB). Mary

knew instantly that Elizabeth's pregnancy was miraculous, and that she would have someone else with whom to share this miraculous birth journey. The angel Gabriel had also visited Zachariah to reveal Elizabeth's pregnancy, and the role of their future son and the coming Messiah. After hearing the news, Mary hurried to visit Elizabeth. Their encounter shows the joy and provision of God.

When Elizabeth heard Mary's greeting, the baby leaped inside her, and Elizabeth was filled with the Holy Spirit. Then she exclaimed with a loud cry: "You are the most blessed of women, and your child will be blessed!" (Luke 1:41-42 HCSB).

Mary and Elizabeth shared joy in their pregnancies and in the idea of their sons' futures together. We can only imagine their conversations: Will we be good mothers? What will our sons be like? How will our sons be received by the world? Mary stayed with Elizabeth for about three months. They had time to discuss, pray, and support each other in their pregnancies. Mary and Elizabeth's journey confirms that God will also provide the right people to support you in your purpose.

Provision Through Protection

The gospel of Matthew illustrates God's provision through protection over Jesus and His family. After the birth of Jesus, many heard of His miraculous birth and sought to see the Messiah, the Redeemer of Israel, and the King of the Jews. *Wise Men*, who were believed to be astrologers, traveled to Jerusalem led by a star to seek and worship the new King. However the excitement of the new "*King of the Jews*," disturbed King Herod. A new King posed a threat to him. Because he was threatened by the coming Messiah, King Herod summoned the wise men and inquired about their visit. He then directed them to find the child, and report back to him.

However, King Herod had ulterior motives and planned to harm Jesus.

Following the star, the Wise Men found Jesus and His family. They immediately fell to their knees in worship as they presented gifts to Him. Their gifts signified Jesus' royal status. The gold, frankincense, and myrrh together were gifts that represent a King worthy of worship. After their time of worshiping Jesus, the Wise Men were warned in a dream not to return to Herod, so they took another route back to their own country. After the Wise Men left for their own country, an angel warned Joseph in a dream:

Get up! Take the child and His mother, flee to Egypt, and stay there until I tell you. For Herod is about to search for the child to destroy Him (Matthew 2: 13 HCSB).

When Herod saw that the Wise Men did not return, he ordered all male children in the area of Bethlehem two years old and younger to be killed. Herod's actions fulfilled the prophesy of Jeremiah, stating that many tribes of Israel would die and there would be a great mourning. However, God used the Wise Men and the angel to warn Joseph and give Jesus and His family time to flee to safety. After Herod died, an angel appeared to Joseph once again and instructed him to return to the land of Israel. Mary and Joseph then *went and settled in a town called Nazareth to fulfill what was spoken through the prophets, that He will be called a Nazarene* (Matthew 2:23 HCSB).

Mary and Joseph continued to see God's provision throughout their lives. God's faithfulness towards them shows us that when we are following and pursuing the will of God, He is there also. Not only will God be with you along the way, He has already blessed you as His chosen heir. God has bestowed power upon you to be successful in your purpose. Mary's life illustrates how God can exalt the lowly and equip the inadequate to accomplish His plan and purpose for our lives. Like Mary, we must be willing to surrender our will to God. When we give ourselves completely to the will of God, He will respond by providing all you need to accomplish His will.

Spiritual Discipline in Action

This exchange of faith over fear is a consistent battle for all of us. I only imagine the fear Mary experienced while carrying Jesus Christ, the Savior of the world in her womb. However, Mary knew Scripture. Mary not only knew the Old Testament prophesies of the promised Messiah, but she found peace in them. The Word of God should be a source of confidence and peace to us as well.

I remember considering to embark on my first mission trip to Ghana, West Africa. I would travel to Ghana and be there for two weeks with the purpose of helping provide youth in the disadvantage area of Mamprobi- Accra, Ghana with opportunities to succeed in both academics and sports. I had this great idea, but how was I going to accomplish it? I had no clue, all I knew was God placed this mission trip on my heart, and He would provide a way. I needed to raise funds for my flight and the supplies I would provide to the children. Oh, and by the way I had just started my new job with a professional sports team. So, if I took the time off, it would be unpaid leave. So, in addition to raising funds for the trip, I also had to consider how my rent and other monthly expenses were going to be paid.

Continuing to exchange faith over fear, I stepped out and created a fundraising campaign. I asked everyone I knew. I even partnered with a local church to allow donors to receive receipts for taxes. Funds were raised for the flight and school supplies, and shoes were collected. However, I still had no clue how my monthly expenses were going to be covered. Then I remembered the verse that encouraged me to take this trip in the first place.

Be strong and courageous. Do not be afraid or terrified because of them, for the LORD your God goes with you; he will never leave you nor forsake you (Deuteronomy 31:6).

God wanted me to trust Him. God wanted me to trust how He had bestowed power upon me to succeed. God wanted me to learn that when He calls, He also provides. I found peace in this verse, but I had no clue how God would provide.

We hosted a special event for our season ticket holders, my last day of work. We allowed them to sit in seats, walk on the arena floor, and handpick their new seats. This day I had one client planning to attend the event, and I had one chance to make a sale and earn commission. But . . . he called saying he was sick and needed to cancel. So I started to think how I would cover bills with the limited credit on my credit card. I started to think how my aunt who co-signed on my car was going to be upset with me if I missed a payment. I started to think that maybe this trip was a mistake.

But God . . . God had a different plan. My client showed up and bought season tickets. Not just any season tickets, but courtside seats worth $84,000. The commission itself covered the trip, my monthly expenses, and I could also pay off my car! "Wow, God you are so good and faithful!" I exclaimed. My client shared how impressed he was with my service and felt he needed to show up at the event. He was even more excited to learn about my trip. I share this story because God will prove Himself faithful, if we respond with a yes. I had no idea how God was going to provide, but He provided beyond what I could ever imagine.

And the provision didn't stop there. When I returned to work, I was excited to receive my commission check. However, there were two checks. One check for my commission, and the other was from vacation hours donated by my co-workers! When God tells you to trust Him, He means He will be there for each and every step you take. Like Mary, God provided all I needed to accomplish the good work He created me to do. The spiritual discipline of *Bible study* helped me to apply the Word of God to my everyday life. When I applied the Word of God to my life, God responded in a mighty way. I encourage you to allow the Word of God to transform your life as an heir to God's Image.

Discipline—*Bible Study*

Purpose: To engage with Scripture in order to understand the Word of God and apply its truth and power to everyday life.

Read these Scriptures and answer the following questions:
- Jeremiah 1:4- 8
- Exodus 3:10 & 4:10-12

1. The two passages speak of Jeremiah and Moses. What do these two men have in common?

2. What has God asked of them? What is their response to God?

3. What is God's response? How does God's response make you feel?

4. What does God's response reveal about His charac-
    ter? How can you apply God's response to Mary, Jer-
    emiah, and Moses to your own life?

Chapter Overview

1. You are an *heiress*! We are the beneficiary of God's
    image and likeness, which makes us His *Image Bear-
    ers*. These blessings are an inheritance given from
    God the Father to His children.

2. Today's understanding of an inheritance centers on
    the person receiving the fortune. However, a true in-
    heritance actually has nothing to do with the person
    receiving the inheritance; but centers on the giver.
    We must keep our heritance "God centered."

3. We must trust that God blesses His creation with all
    we need to successfully fulfill our purpose as His Im-
    age Bearers.

4. Mary was 14 years old when God invited her to
    mother the "Son of God"; not knowing what was to
    come, Mary trusted God.

5. Because of Mary's trust and willingness, God pro-
    vided for her through Joseph, Elizabeth, the Wise
    Men, and the angels.

6. Like Mary we must be willing to give ourselves
    wholly to the will of God in order to live in our worth.

Related Scriptures

- Jeremiah 29:11
- Acts 20:32
- Colossians 1:12

CHAPTER 3

Created to Relate

I have loved you with an everlasting love; Therefore
I have continued my faithfulness to you
(Jeremiah 31:3 ESV).

We have inherited the image of God, of all creation; mankind is the only creation that bears the image of God. How does it feel to know God chose you to bear His Image? That He chose you to be a representative of His might, wisdom, and love? Inheriting the image of God makes me really know how God truly feels about me. How He trusts me with this great inheritance and how He finds me worthy to receive it. I want you to know that we not only *inherit* worth as *Image Bearers*, but we are also *assigned* worth with responsibility. Like Mary, Jeremiah, and Moses, God has called us all to bear His image responsibly. The responsibilities of our inheritance are to relate, reflect, and reign; to relate with God and others, to Reflect His image, and to Reign over the earth. In this chapter we learn how we were created to relate.

The Nature of Our Inheritance

The creation story reveals the process of God's creative work. It unveils the intimate details of God creating and giving. God gives of His image and likeness to His most valued creation.

> *Then the Lord God formed a man from the dust of the ground and breathed into his nostrils the breath of life, and the man became a living being (Genesis 2:7 NIV).*

God *created* the heavens and the earth while He *formed* mankind. The word *formed* expresses relationship and intimacy between the creator and the created. As God gives of His image and likeness, we inherit the ability to *relate* to God and others. This reveals God's desire to go deeper with the creation He intimately formed. For this reason, the first blessing or task of our inheritance is to *relate*. We have already learned that God's image includes the ability to communicate and fellowship. We will now discover how God's image also includes rational, volitional, and moral capacities for humans to serve responsibly as God's *Image Bearers*. Let's take a look at how we are wired for relationship with God and to others.

Wired for Relationship
It is not good for the man to be alone (Genesis 2:18 NIV).

Adam was the first of his kind. Adam had a fruitless search for an equal companion who shared his intellect, reasoning, and moral abilities. Adam knew something significant was missing from his life, but did not know for sure what he was looking for. It is important to note that God did not complete mankind until Adam realized he was insufficient without a proper helpmate. Eve was created to fulfill a need of companionship, and to enhance life through co-rulership. Adam was amazed at Eve's beauty, but even more thrilled that he had found his equal. Eve was the companion Adam was searching for. He could communicate with her, understand her, and share his purpose and blessings with her. God sanctioned their union and they complemented each other perfectly. Adam and Eve were one as God is one.

God Desires for Us to Be One

In the book of John, Jesus prays for all of His believers. He prays they will be one in unity, so the world may believe in Him. Our inheritance to *relate* to God and others honors God. Let's see how:

> *I pray not only for these, but also for those who believe in Me through their message. May they all be one, as You, Father, are in Me and I am in You. May they also be one in Us, so the world may believe You sent Me. I have given them the glory You have given Me. May they be one as We are one. I am in them and You are in Me. May they be made completely one, so the world may know You have sent Me and have loved them as You have loved Me (John 17:20-23 HCSB).*

Jesus prays for believers to be unified as one, so the world may believe God is real. *So the world may know You sent me* is repeated throughout this passage to emphasize its importance. The repetition also highlights our role in God's plan for salvation. When love and joy is expressed in our human relationships it benefits more than those involved. "Seeing [our] benevolence, charity, and holy joy, the people of the world, the carnal part of mankind, may believe that a religion productive of such amiable fruits is indeed of divine origin."[3] When we keep our heritance to *relate* "God centered," we can't help but bring honor and glory to our benefactor.

Reflection Questions
1. If everyone viewed themselves and others as "Image Bearers," how differently do you think we would treat each other?

2. Knowing that unity in relationships brings honor to God, how will you strive to bring unity in your relationships?

As Adam and Eve grew closer to each other, they learned more about the image in which they were created. They enjoyed the world's first marriage and experienced the deepest connection of any creation of God. They lived in paradise and life was easy. However, Adam and Eve quickly learned their most important relationship was their relationship with God.

A Broken Relationship

As rational creatures, Adam and Eve were also able to fellowship with God. God created mankind, so he could communicate his thoughts, feelings, and petitions to Him. They were able to know their creator intimately; know His thoughts as well as His standards. God gave Adam and Eve simple instructions: Be fruitful and multiply, subdue and rule over the earth, and do not eat of the tree of *The Knowledge of Good and Evil*. This deep intimacy shared between mankind and God was called into question when Eve was deceived into doubting God and His Word.

God's Command

The Lord God took the man and put him in the Garden of Eden to work it and take care of it. And the Lord God commanded the man, "You are free to eat from any tree in the garden; but you must not eat from the tree of the knowledge of good and evil, for when you eat from it you will certainly die" (Genesis 2:15-17).

Mankind's Response

Now the serpent was more crafty than any of the wild animals the Lord God had made. He said to the woman, "Did God really say, 'You must not eat from any tree in the garden'?" The woman said to the serpent, "We may eat fruit from the trees in the garden, but God did say, 'You must not eat fruit from the tree that is in the middle of the garden, and you must not touch it, or you will die.'" "You will not certainly die," the serpent said to the woman. "For God knows that when you eat from it your eyes will be opened, and you will be like God, knowing good and evil" (Genesis 3:1-5).

The verses above depict the story of *The Fall* of mankind from holiness. *The Fall* notes the first and original transgression against God. *"When the woman saw that the fruit of the tree was good for food and pleasing to the eye, and also desirable for gaining wisdom, she took some and ate it. She also gave some to her husband, who was with her, and he ate it"* (Genesis 3:6 NIV). We see that Satan deceived Eve but Adam willfully rebelled against God. Adam and Eve felt the consequences of their sin against God immediately. They felt shame and fear before the holiness of God and hid from Him. When presented with an opportunity to confess their transgression, Adam and Eve tried to cover their sin by casting the blame on Satan.

Reflection Questions
Read Genesis 3: 7-13 and answer the following questions:

1. The serpent deceived Eve and Adam willfully rebelled. What are the differences in their roles in disobeying God?

2. Why did Adam and Eve hide from God?

3. What does their nakedness represent? Why did their nakedness bring on the urge to cover themselves and hide from God?

Adam and Eve were given all of the land, but were asked not to eat from one tree. Where did Adam and Eve go wrong? How could they desire more? God had given them all they would ever need! The problem was Adam and Eve mishandled their inheritance to *relate* in two ways: Mistrust and independence. Satan brought doubt into the minds of mankind by questioning God's motives. *"Did he really say"* . . . *"You will not die"* . . . *"You will be like God"* are the phrases Satan used to deny God's goodness. Satan made Adam and Eve believe God's prohibitions were simply to withhold power from them, and not to protect them.

Mistrust and Independence

Mankind negated what they knew about God—His sovereignty, wisdom, and provision and settled for half-truths. Eve displayed her mistrust of God's goodness by failing to believe God commands what is good and profitable.

Eve viewed prohibitions as if God was withholding a good thing from her, not protecting her. This mistrust also led to a disbelief in the consequence of sin. God had warned the penalty of sin was death, but Satan convinced Eve she would *be like God, knowing good and evil.* "Satan tempted Eve at the same point at which he himself had fallen, the desire to usurp the prerogatives of God."[4]

As a result Adam and Eve both acted independently of God. Adam and Eve submitted to their own desires, instead of the will of God. This act of independence neglected their most important relationship, impacting the human condition before God. Instead of righteousness and oneness with God, sin brought human guilt and shame, and a marred reflection of the image of God. This marred image, spiritual and moral corruption, separated mankind from God. Today we still suffer from these consequences. Chapter 4 will explain how our inheritance to relate can be reclaimed and restored. Meanwhile, take time to reflect upon your relationship with God and others.

Reflection Questions

1. What areas in your life are difficult to completely trust God?

2. Adam and Eve made a big decision independent of God. What life decisions have you made independent of God? What were the results of those decisions?

3. What steps can you take to begin including God in your decision-making?

Spiritual Discipline in Action

God desires a relationship with us. He created us in His likeness, and relationship is at the core of our purpose. "Made in God's image, humans are incomplete until they find themselves in relationship to the God who created them for intimate communion with himself. For Christians, this is the ultimate meaning and purpose of life."[5] Many preach about having a relationship with God, but many do not give practical ways to develop a relationship with God. I work with young Christians every day, and this is a hot topic of discussion. Many want to know: How do I develop a relationship with God? How do I know I have a good relationship with God?

Let's say you were interested in entering a romantic relationship. What would you do to get to know that person? How would you express your interest? Would you make time for them or express how special they are to you? As we think about these questions, many of our answers will also pertain to building a relationship with God. So, let's begin to make a list: Spend time with them, get to know them, find out what they like, present your best self to them, do what they like to do, etc.

How can we translate these principles to God? Are we spending time with Him, through prayer and reading His Word? Are we getting to know what He likes through attending church and studying the Bible? Do we desire to make time for Him? Is He a priority in lives? Many of us have friends we can spend a substantial amount of time away from, but when we reconnect it's like we never missed a beat. But what if I spent three months away from my husband and didn't speak to him? How do you think this would impact our relationship? I would feel so disconnected to Him, I would even wonder about the status of our relationship. Are we still together? Will this still work?

I believe our relationship with God is like the latter. We need to spend quality time with God. He desires to spend time with us, and provides ways for us to communicate and grow in relationship with Him. God also knows we are sinful in nature, and when we repent before Him; He allows us to be forgiven. He provides ways for us to restore our relationship with Him through confessing our sin towards Him. The spiritual discipline of *Self-Examination and Confession* allows us to admit our faults to God and to embrace the gift of forgiveness. Let's take a few moments to examine ourselves before God.

Discipline—*Self-Examination and Confession*
Purpose: To admit faults and shortcomings to God, to embrace the gift of forgiveness and restoration, to be set on a path of change and regeneration.

Adam and Eve failed to trust God's goodness and disobeyed His command not to eat of the *Tree of the Knowledge of Good and Evil*. Because of their initial sin, we as descendants of Adam have inherited a fall from righteousness. Adam and Eve's fall from righteousness was rooted in mistrust and independence. Self- examination and confession will allow us to gain insight into our own personal temptations to later have victory over them.

Take 30 min to complete the following:
1. Read Psalm 51. Reflect on the phrases that stick out to you.

2. Read the following Scriptures. Notice how they define sin: Galatians 5:19-21, Proverbs 6:16-19, and Colossians 3:8-10. Take 15 minutes to journal and confess the sins you have committed.

3.   Finally, reflect and journal your thoughts on the possible root of those sins (e.g. Roots can be the following: Mistrust, independence, selfishness, bitterness, anger, etc.).

Chapter Overview

1.   We not only *inherit* worth as *Image Bearers*, but are also *assigned* worth with responsibility to Relate to God and others, Reflect His image, and Reign over the earth.

2.   When we keep our heritage to relate "God centered," we can't help but bring honor and glory to our benefactor.

3.   However, the deep intimacy shared between mankind and God was called into question when Eve was deceived into doubting God and His Word.

4.   Adam and Eve mishandled their inheritance to *relate* in two ways: Mistrust and independence. Mankind negated what they knew about God, His sovereignty, wisdom, and provision; and settled for half-truths.

5.   Instead of righteousness and oneness with God, sin brought guilt and a marred reflection of the image of God. This marred image, spiritual and moral corruption, separated mankind from God.

Related Scriptures

- Psalms 103:13-14
- Matthew 6:6
- Galatians 4:6
- Jeremiah 29:12-13

Created to Reflect

Bring to me all the people who are mine, whom
I made for my glory, whom I formed and made
(Isaiah 43:7, NCV).

Y ou were created to be an Image Bearer of God, created to reflect the image and likeness of your Creator, and created to be a representative of Him on
earth. Before sin entered the world, Adam and Eve
reflected the fullest image of God mankind could possibly reflect. Sin and disobedience affected their relationship with
God by damaging their reflection of God. Mankind no longer
represented the holiness or righteousness of God. Instead, the
image of God was blemished; they reflected a fractured image. "The image of God in fallen humanity is like an encased
mirror that holds broken and misaligned pieces. The mirror
reflects remnants of the fractured image.[6] Like the mirror we
continue to reflect fragments of God's image; however sin re-
stricts our ability to reflect God properly.

How can we restore our reflection? How can we reclaim our inheritance to reflect the image of God properly?
In this chapter we will examine the problem of sin and God's
solution to restore our inheritance.

What Does It Mean to Reflect the Image of God?

As an Image Bearer of God, we inherit the task of reflecting God. We were created to reflect the image of God, but we need to know what this truly means. Reflecting the image of God does not mean to look like God or to sit pretty as one of God's most esthetic works. Reflecting encompasses responsibility and importance. The word *reflect* means to show something, to make something known, and to show an image. To reflect the image of God means to show who He is, to make Him known. It is our purpose to live in a way that makes God known to the world around us. We were created to show the world who God really is. We were created to show the world God's holiness, wisdom, love, and dominion. Unfortunately, sin inhibits our ability to complete the assigned task as Image Bearers. Let's now take a look at the problem of sin.

The Problem of Sin

Surely the arm of the Lord is not too short to save, nor his ear too dull to hear. But your iniquities have separated you from your God; your sins have hidden his face from you, so that he will not hear (Isaiah 59: 1-2).

Sins are actions, thoughts, or attitudes that are outside the character of God. Sin is rebellion against God, rebellion against His holiness and authority. Sin literally means, "missing the mark," the mark of God's holy perfection. Sin is detrimental to the human condition because of sin's numerous consequences. Sin results in guilt, shame, and bondage. Sin has physical, psychological, and spiritual consequences. Adam and Eve were warned that sin leads to death. They were told if they ate of the forbidden tree, *they would surely die*.

Adam and Eve suffered the immediate consequence of a spiritual death. After they ate of the tree, Adam and Eve's *eyes were opened* and they realized their nakedness. They immediately felt the effects of sin and sought to cover their sin by covering their nakedness. When approached by God, they hid from God. When asked about their actions, they pointed fingers. Adam blamed Eve, and Eve blamed the serpent. Ultimately Adam and Eve's decision to act independently of God separated them from God.

Geography Class

While we still reflect bits and pieces of the image of God, sin disfigures the image we reflect of God. Sin also interrupts the purpose for which we were created. Kristen learned how sin not only separated her from God but from her purpose in one unlikely illustration. Kristen was raised in a Christian home and was taught to love God with all of her heart, soul, mind, and strength. However when it came to romantic relationships, she excluded God from the selection process. Kristen was left with a trail of bad relationships and a broken heart. She continued to settle and comprise her values to make relationships work, and her last relationship left her with more than just a broken heart. Kristen was now a sophomore in college and pregnant. While contemplating her next steps, Kristen continued to go to class and had an "ah ha" moment in one of her General Ed courses.

World Geography helped Kristen understand sin better than any sermon or Bible study. Her professor explained how if a plane departing from Los Angeles in route to Honolulu, Hawaii, gets off course by 1 degree during the duration of the flight, the plane might end up in the Philippines. Kristen began to feel overwhelming warmth move within her body. She knew God was speaking to her through "geography," a class she didn't want to take, but fulfilled her GE requirements. She thought to herself, "I have drifted, I'm in the freaking Philippines." One careless decision always seemed to lead to another. "Compromise and settling has completely gotten me off course!"

Like Adam and Eve, Kristen faced the consequences of her sin. Kristen decided to keep her unborn child and would be a single mother. Kristen also left school the following semester. She and her unborn child would face the reality of sin and how sin separates us from God. Spiritual separation has corrupted and brought devastation to our human nature. Mankind also holds the negative guilt of sin and moral separation. Adam's corrupt nature was transferred to his descendants. God is good; mankind is not. *For all have sinned and fall short of the glory of God* (Romans 3:23). Therefore we all suffer eternal separation from God.

However Kristen's story, as well as Adam and Eve's story, does not end with sin and consequences. God offers a solution to redeem His precious creation from sin.

God's Solution

God's holiness and righteousness could not allow sin to go unpunished. But God is also loving and compassionate and could not allow us to be eternally separated from Him. God provided a remedy for the sin of Adam and Eve. God covered Adam and Eve's spiritual and moral nakedness with garments of "animal skin" (Genesis 3:21). Adam and Eve attempted to clothes themselves and cover their guilt, but they learned that only God could cover and forgive their sin. God sacrificed an innocent animal to cover them and atone for their disobedience. The garments of animal skin represented righteousness provided by God, so Adam and Eve could stand in His holy presence.

Sacrifice

The sacrifice of the animal was a prelude to the once-and for- all sacrifice of Christ. Jesus, Mary's baby, would be God's divine solution for sin. Even the first book of the Bible, Genesis, prophesies of Christ's defeat over Satan and sin.

I will put hostility between you and the woman, and be-
tween your seed and her seed. He will Strike your head,
and you will strike his heel (Genesis 3:15 HCSB).

Her seed, Eve's descendant, would strike the head of
Satan, delivering a fatal blow to defeat death and the power
of sin. Jesus Christ was born for this very reason, to *save his*
people from their sin (Matthew 1:21). God gave His only Son,
born of a virgin, to live a sinless life, and be the sacrifice for
sin.

God presented Christ as a sacrifice of atonement,
through the shedding of his blood—to be received by
faith. He did this to demonstrate his righteousness, be-
cause in his forbearance he had left the sins committed
beforehand unpunished (Romans 3:25).

Substitution

The sacrifice of Jesus Christ offers a permanent solution for sin. Jesus pays the penalty of sin for us; Christ stands
in our place for our punishment.   Jesus, the Son of God, was
the only person qualified to be a substitution, for only God
can save, but man also had to pay for their sin. Christ as fully
God and fully man came into the world to complete the mission of redemption. God the Father warned the penalty of sin
was death, and Jesus died to pay that penalty. Jesus was crucified on a cross and took on Himself the sin of the world.

God made him who had no sin to be sin for us, so that in
him we might become the righteousness of God
(2 Corinthians 5:21).

The death of Christ became our eternal covering for
sin. The "once and for all" sacrifice of Christ's life allows us

to stand before God clothed in righteousness. The righteousness of Christ is imputed to us. This means the righteousness of Christ is accredited to us when we believe in the gospel of Christ. The word *gospel* means good news. The gospel of Christ means there is "good news" in God's solution for sin. God the Father gave His only Son as a substitute for our punishment. The gospel can be summed up in this one verse:

> *For God so loved the world that he gave his one and only Son, that whoever believes in him shall not perish but have eternal life (John 3:16).*

Reflection Questions

1. The holiness of God moved Him to punish sin. What moves God to provide a solution for sin?

2. Why is Jesus the only suitable sacrifice for sin?

3. The Bible teaches that Jesus Christ was the God-man, fully God and fully human. Why did God's once-and-for-all sacrifice need to be fully human and fully God?

4. Jesus was a human being, born of a virgin and the Holy Spirit. Why did God need to use a virgin to rear the Son of God? (Think in terms of a sinless sacrifice).

Salvation

The death of Christ pays the penalty for our sin. Christ took our place, to appease the wrath of God. His death allows our reflection and relationship with God to be fully reconciled. We know the sacrifice of Christ was acceptable to God the Father because of the resurrection of Christ. Christ defeated death and rose from the dead three days after he was crucified.

This is what is written: The Messiah will suffer and rise from the dead on the third day, and repentance for the forgiveness of sins will be preached in his name to all nations, beginning at Jerusalem (Luke 24:46-47).

For we know that since Christ was raised from the dead, he cannot die again; death no longer has mastery over him. The death he died, he died to sin once for all; but the life he lives, he lives to God (Romans 6:9-10).

The resurrection is essential to the gospel or Good News of Christ because it is through faith in Christ that we are saved from the punishment of sin. Salvation is deliverance. It is the act of being saved from sin's punishment, spiritual darkness, and eternal separation from God. The Bible teaches we are saved through grace, not by any work of our own hands. We are like Adam and Eve, who could not cover their own sin or make themselves righteous to stand in the holy presence of God. We are saved by the gift of grace when we believe in what Jesus Christ has already done on the cross. Grace is *unmerited favor* or goodwill we receive from God. God gives this gift of grace because of His love and compassion towards us. Grace provides a solution for sin.

> *If you confess with your mouth, "Jesus is Lord," and believe in your heart that God raised Him from the dead, you will be saved. One believes with the heart, resulting in righteousness, and one confesses with the mouth, resulting in salvation (Romans 10:9-10 HCSB).*

God's salvation plan includes three stages: *past salvation, present salvation, and future salvation. Past salvation* means God has already paid the penalty for past, present, and future sin. *Present salvation* refers to how God continues to save us from the power of sin over our lives as we live day-to-day. Lastly, *future salvation* means that at the return of Christ, believers will be glorified and conformed to Christ's perfect image. God is actively saving us and has provided a solution for sin. This is truly great news.

Our Response

Salvation is a gift from God. Our loving and compassionate God made the ultimate sacrifice to restore our relationship with Him and to restore our reflection of Him. *But now in Christ Jesus you who once were far away have been brought near by the blood of Christ* (Ephesians 2:13 HCSB). Christ has bridged the gap that once separated us from God. Now all we have to do is believe. The Bible teaches that if we confess with our mouth that Jesus is Lord and believe in our heart that He rose from the dead, and then we will be saved (Romans 10:9-10).

Will you accept this gift? Will you open your heart to receive a gift that has no strings attached? Will you accept a gift from a loving heavenly Father that wants a relationship with you? All of the work has been done; now you simply must believe. Christ took on your sin so the Father could see you in your true light.

When we believe in the sacrifice and resurrection of Christ, we no longer reflect a fragmented image of God. We reflect Him correctly when we believe. When we believe Jesus Christ took on our sin, His righteousness is accredited to us. When God looks at us, He sees the righteousness of Christ. When God looks at you, He doesn't see your mistakes, guilt, or shame: He sees your best! Christ died so you could be your best self.

Christ died so you wouldn't have to live in the consequences of sin, but in your divine purpose as an Image Bearer. Christ died so you could see yourself the way God sees you. **Christ died because you are worth it!**

Prayer for Salvation

If you are ready to receive the free gift of salvation, please pray this prayer:

*Heavenly Father, I have sinned and have
fallen short of your glory.
Sin has separated me from you and I ask for forgiveness.
I thank you for sending your Son to die for my sin.
I thank you for paying the penalty for my sin.
I believe that Jesus Christ is your one and only Son.
I believe that He is the Savior of the world, and I believe
you raised Him from the dead.
I receive you as head of my life and I receive your gift of salvation.
Please guide my life, and help me to reflect your Image correctly to the world.
-Amen*

If you have sincerely prayed this prayer, the Bible promises you are a new creation in Christ. *Therefore, if anyone is in Christ, he is a new creation; old things have passed away, and look, new things have come* (2 Corinthians 5:17, HCSB). You are made new in Christ, and you must see yourself in this manner. You must see yourself as a new creation that is forgiven and set free to live in your worth and purpose in Christ.

The Rest of the Story

Do you remember Kristen? Her story didn't end with sin and consequences, but redemption. When Kristen left school the following semester, she gave birth to her son Aden. Kristen rededicated her life to Christ and began helping other women not to make the mistakes she made. Kristen went back to school and continued on to post-graduate studies. Today Kristen's son is 9 years old and Kristen is a Social Worker, working to help restore young women and families to their purpose and worth in Christ. Although Kristen drifted, with God she could be placed back on course. Kristen's response to the "good news" allowed her to reclaim her purpose and calling, now she wants to help others live the life they were created to live.

Like Kristen, all believers are called to relate and reflect the image of God. In the next chapter we will learn more about our call to reign.

Spiritual Discipline in Action

Discipline—*Prayer of Recollection*
Purpose: Prayer of recollection connects us to the reality of who we are in Christ. It allows us to heal from our past sin and fragmented reflection of God. Prayer of recollection is to remind us of *grace* and *forgiveness,* so we can move towards our true identity in Christ.

I Felt New

"Ty, I know it may sound weird, but I felt new, like a new creation," said Lauren. I assured Lauren it wasn't weird, and in fact my heart was overjoyed to hear her say she felt like a new creation. I've counseled Lauren for years, and repeatedly reminded her of the faithfulness of God. How that when we confess our sins, He is faithful to forgive. How God doesn't hold grudges. However, Lauren was plagued by guilt and shame from her past. She had an abortion and in many ways felt God could punish her at any moment. The anniversary of her abortion also reminded her of the loss and guilt of her past. Not only was she grieving, but she never felt worthy of forgiveness.

To hear Lauren say she felt "new, she felt like a new creation" displays the good news of Christ. It's not about what we've done, but all about what God has done for us. Christ died because she was worth forgiving. The spiritual discipline of prayer of recollection helps us to speak of the reality of our identity in Christ. Even if we don't quite believe it yet, we need to remind ourselves of God's grace.

Take 10 minutes to fill out characteristics of your old self and new self. Use the following Scriptures to help guide your list.

Old Self
Romans 6:23, Isaiah 59:2, and Colossians 1:21

1. Dead in Sin_____

2. _____

3. _____

4. _____

5. _____

New Self
Ephesians 2:13, Psalm 103:12, and Galatians 3:26

1. <u>New Creation</u>_____

2. _____

3. _____

4. _____

5. _____

Take 15 minutes to pray for God to help you identify and live in your new identity in Christ. If you have doubts or disbelief, ask God to help you grow in faith in His Son and in true forgiveness.

Chapter Overview

1. Before sin entered their lives, Adam and Eve reflected the fullest image of God that mankind could possibly reflect.

2. We were created to reflect the Image of God. The word *reflect* means: to show something, to make something known, and to show an image. To reflect the image of God means to show who He is. To reflect the image of God means to make Him known.

3. Unfortunately, sin inhibits our ability to complete the assigned task as Image Bearers; let's take a look at the problem of sin.

4. God is also loving and compassionate towards us and could not allow us to be punished eternally because of sin.

5. God's solution for sin is the sacrifice and substitution of Christ.

6. There is salvation in Christ. Christ's death and resurrection pays the penalty of our sin.

7. Belief in Christ allows our sin to be forgiven, and allows us to be a new creation in Him.

Related Scriptures

- Luke 23:26-49
- John 3:16; Romans 6:22
- 1 Corinthians 7:23
- Romans 5:9
- 2 Corinthians 6:2

CHAPTER 5

Created to Reign

This saying is trustworthy: For if we have died with Him,
we will also live with Him; if we endure,
we will Also reign with Him
(2 Timothy 2:11-12a HCSB).

The "once and for all" sacrifice of Christ satisfied the penalty of sin. We have been saved from the penalty of sin that leads to death. Because Christ lives, we live. The resurrection of Christ redeems us from spiritual darkness and bondage to sin. The resurrection restores us to a proper relationship with God and repairs our broken image of Him. Finally, the resurrection of Christ allows us to *reign*. Our inheritance to *Reign* is at the core of our purpose on earth and is at the core of the image and likeness in which we were created.

Created to Rule

When we think of world reign or rule, we may think of kings ruling or royalty. We may not think of ourselves as royalty, kings or queens, but God created us for this very purpose. We were created to rule over creation. We learned in Genesis 1:26-31 how God blessed His creation and commissioned mankind to *rule* and *subdue* the earth. We were to rule over the earth as a representative of God and to rule in such a way that brought Him glory. The New Testament also testifies of our royal purpose:

But you are a chosen people, a royal priesthood, a holy nation, God's special possession, that you may declare the praises of him who called you out of darkness into his wonderful light (1 Peter 2:9).

The apostle Peter penned the purpose of those who are restored in Christ. He called us a "royal priesthood," which means we are a body of kingly priests with access to God through Christ. Before the resurrection of Christ, God's people could not confess their sin or receive forgiveness without a priest. Sin separated us from God's holy presence and the priest served as a mediator or bridge between God and the people. However, Christ changed all of this. Christ is now our High Priest and serves as our mediator to the Father. Because of Christ we can now approach God and share intimacy with Him.

Intimacy is why God calls us a "chosen people" and His "special possession." A plan for salvation was so important to God because we are special to Him. We are God's prized possession, and He was willing to do whatever it took to save us. The sacrifice of His only Son proves our importance to God. God desired for His special possession to function in its true purpose and through Christ, accomplish our original purpose to relate, reflect, and reign. In sin we lost our purpose, but through Christ we can reclaim it.

"Ah Ha" Moment

Sometimes after leading a Campus Bible study full of blank stares from teenagers, I am not sure if they hear a word I am saying. At times it can be disheartening to pour out your heart and plea with youth to put their trust in Christ; just to hear the school bell ring and a rush towards the door. However, one day a girl named Remy stayed to talk after the bell.

She shared how the message seemed to be just for her. She felt God did not hear her prayers and she simply felt insignificant to God. Remy struggled with bouts of depression and tried her best to pray her way out of it. Nothing seemed to work and she felt God was real but not present in her life. She felt God could answer prayers, just not her prayers.

Remy went on to say "I have been called out of darkness into light" touched my heart in a special way. "I need to live in the truth of who I am in Christ" Remy replied. What's funny about this encounter with Remy is that the message I spoke had nothing to do with the revelation she just shared with me. What I thought fell on deaf ears spoke to Remy, even when it wasn't what I said at all!

So I went on and shared 1 Peter 2:9 with Remy. That yes, she has been called out of darkness in to light because she is chosen and a special possession to God. Hearing how she was a special possession to God helped Remy see the root to much of her sadness. She felt insignificant to her parents and now God because her prayers weren't being answered. Remy was late to her next class, however she had a breakthrough and a heart encounter with Christ. She felt significant to God!

Reflection Questions

1. You are a "royal priesthood" chosen to declare the glory of God. How do you feel about adding the title of priest or minister to your name? Would you ever consider yourself a minister? What do you believe your roles or duties as a priest would be?

2. God calls you His "special possession." Before reading 1 Peter 2:9, have you ever considered yourself as special to God? What steps or actions can you take to remind yourself daily that you are special to God?

Anointed to Reign

Now it is God who makes both us and you stand firm in Christ. He anointed us, set his seal of ownership on us, and put his Spirit in our hearts as a deposit, guaranteeing what is to come (2 Corinthians 1:21-22).

To anoint means to bless for divine service. Both the Old and New Testaments note examples of physical and spiritual anointing. Kings were anointed to rule, like our example of David who was anointed by Samuel. Prophets like Jeremiah were anointed to proclaim the Word of God. Priests were also anointed to fulfill their duties of worship and sacrifice. Often times the anointing took place by the pouring of oil upon one's head for the purpose of grooming or bestowing spiritual ability for a divine cause. Jesus, however, was anointed a bit differently. Let's take a look at the anointing of Jesus.

Then Jesus came from Galilee to the Jordan to be baptized by John . . . .. As soon as Jesus was baptized, he went up out of the water. At that moment heaven was opened, and he saw the Spirit of God descending like a dove and alighting on him. And a voice from heaven said, "This is my Son, whom I love; with him I am well pleased" (Matthew 3:13, 16-17).

First Jesus' name provides the purpose for His anointing. Christ or *Christos* in Greek means, "Anointed one" where Jesus or *Yeshua* in the Hebrew means "Yahweh (God) saves." Jesus would be anointed to save us, to be the Savior of the world. The Holy Spirit anointed Jesus at His baptism. The Bible depicts how the Spirit of God descended upon Christ as a dove, and this marked the beginning of His ministry. After His baptism and anointing, Jesus began to travel and demonstrate His power to overcome temptation, heal the sick, and also to resurrect the dead.

Before the death and resurrection of Christ, Jesus promised believers would receive this same Holy Spirit. He says, *"The Helper, the Holy Spirit, whom the Father will send in my name, he will teach you all things and bring to your remembrance all that I have said to you"* (John 14:26 ESV). Jesus wanted to assure His disciples that in His absence, they would have a Helper in the Holy Spirit. Like Jesus, the Holy Spirit also anoints believers in Christ. This anointing empowers us in many ways like Jesus. The anointing of The Holy Spirit reveals to us the truth of who Christ is and the truth of who we are in Christ. Once we allow the Holy Spirit to reveal the truth of whom we serve and who we are in Christ, we will reign in life.

Reign in Life

In addition to power and kingly rule, the word *reign* also means victory. Like a reigning champion, Christians have victory. Paul asked a simple question in the book of Romans, chapter 8, *If God is for us, who can be against us*? Paul encourages readers by reminding them that God is on their team, and God's team is always a winning team. We reign with Christ! We win with Christ! We are blessed by the Father, redeemed by Christ, and anointed by the Holy Spirit; how can we not be victorious? How can we not reign in life?

> *The thief (Satan) comes only to steal, kill, and destroy. I (Jesus) came that they may have life and have it abundantly (John 10:10 ESV).*

The very sacrifice of Christ was so we may have life. Not just staying alive, but living life fully. Living in your divine purpose, living in joy, and living under the reign of Christ is a full life. When you were in sin, Satan stole your purpose. He fed lies about you and your worth. Satan even fed you lies about the character of God. However, the Holy Spirit has allowed you to know the truth—the truth of how and why you were created and the truth of who created you. Living in God's truth is the ultimate key to seeing yourself the way God sees you.

Reflection Questions

1. Eve believed God's prohibition to eat of the tree was to deny her the right to be like Him. God's warning and rules were actually to protect Adam and Eve. Have you ever believed lies about God or yourself? If so, what were these lies?

2. What truths have you learned about yourself? What truths have you learned about God?

Reign in Holiness

We reign in life when we "reign in holiness." Holiness is not perfection, but simply living in the will of God. We reign in holiness, when we reign over the things that are not of Christ. We reign in holiness when we reign over things that do not bring God glory, and do not reflect His image correctly. With Christ we now have victory over sin and grow in holiness. *For the law of the Spirit of life has set you free in Christ Jesus from the law of sin and death* (Romans 8:2 ESV).

We reign also in the freedom of our salvation. As a new creation in Christ, we may still struggle with sin but sin does not reign over us. Guilt and shame of our past also should not have any power over us. The Bible promises, *if we confess our sins, he is faithful and just to forgive us our sins and to cleanse us from all unrighteousness* (1 John 1:9 ESV). We are forgiven by Christ and set free to live in our purpose. Forgiveness allows us to live in the correct image of God. Before we receive God's gift of salvation, we live in our own image and in our own purpose. When we receive Christ as our Savior, He restores us to live in His image and in His intended purpose for us. We find purpose in holiness; we reign in victory over sin. Let's take a look at a man who lived successfully in his own purpose, until a personal encounter with Christ changed the entire course of his life.

Paul's Story

The apostle Paul is a champion of the Christian faith. He was an apostle, pastor, teacher, missionary, and author. He wrote thirteen books of the New Testament. He lived his Christian life with passion and desired for the entire world to know Christ. Paul was imprisoned for his preaching of the gospel and was also martyred for his faith in Christ. Because of Paul many received Christ, and believers today are still impacted by his testimony.

Paul's testimony includes one of the most well known conversions in the Bible. Paul was born in the city of Tarsus, a metropolis known for trade and excellent universities. Paul was also born into a wealthy Hebrew family. Paul studied under famed Hebrew teacher Gamaliel, and received rabbinical training. He took pride in his culture, calling himself the "Hebrew of Hebrews," and this pride also led to religious pride.

Paul was a member of a strict religious group called the Pharisees. Paul and the Pharisees rejected Jesus as Messiah and rejected His practices. The Pharisees on many occasions attempted to accuse Jesus of breaking Jewish law. The Pharisees disapproved of Jesus because He didn't follow their traditions and He befriended sinners. Paul studied the Old Testament Scriptures that predicted the birth and life of the coming Messiah, yet was completely blinded by religious and cultural pride. The Messiah, the Savior of the world, was in his face, yet Paul persecuted and blasphemed the name of Jesus.

In addition to religious pride, Paul was also a Roman citizen. Paul's Roman citizenship was a passport to travel distant lands with privilege and protection. Roman citizenship was considered a coveted prize in the 1St Century. Roman citizens enjoyed a wide range of benefits and protections. These benefits allowed Paul to travel and spread hate against Jesus and His followers. Paul went house to house persecuting Christians for their faith, even to the point of death. Paul agreed to the killing of Stephen, a deacon of the church, and guarded the clothing of those who murdered him. In fact, Paul, whose Hebrew name was Saul, was on his way to imprison Christians in Damascus, when he encountered Christ.

The Damascus Road

Meanwhile, Saul was still breathing out murderous threats against the Lord's disciples. He went to the high priest and asked him for letters to the synagogues in Damascus, so that if he found any there who belonged to the Way, whether men or women, he might take them as prisoners to Jerusalem. As he neared Damascus on his journey, suddenly a light from heaven flashed around him. He fell to the ground and heard a voice say to him, "Saul, Saul, why do you persecute me?"

"Who are you, Lord?" Saul asked. "I am Jesus, whom you are persecuting," he replied. "Now get up and go into the city, and you will be told what you must do" (Acts 9:1-6).

Paul was blinded by the flash of light for three days and was escorted to Damascus. In Damascus, God spoke to a disciple of Christ named Ananias and instructed him to go to a street called "Straight" to find Saul. Ananias was hesitant because of Saul's persecution of Christians. However, Jesus responded:

"Go! This man is my chosen instrument to proclaim my name to the Gentiles and their kings and to the people of Israel. I will show him how much he must suffer for my name."

Then Ananias went to the house and entered it. Placing his hands on Saul, he said, "Brother Saul, the Lord— Jesus, who appeared to you on the road as you were coming here—has sent me so that you may see again and be filled with the Holy Spirit." Immediately, something like scales fell from Saul's eyes, and he could see again. He got up and was baptized, and after taking some food, he regained his strength.

Saul spent several days with the disciples in Damascus. At once he began to preach in the synagogues that Jesus is the Son of God (Acts 9:15-21).

God's Will

From that point on Paul began to live in his true purpose. Jesus' response to Ananias was that Paul is *my chosen instrument*. Jesus had a great plan for Paul despite his sin. Like Paul, God has chosen you for a unique purpose. Also like Paul, your past is forgiven and will be used for ministry. Paul was a sinner, a murderer, and a persecutor of the faith, yet God pursued him and forgave him. God is pursuing you also to give up your will for His.

Paul believed his Roman citizenship and Hebrew heritage allowed him to reign in life. Yet in reality hate, judgment, and pride reigned over his life. When Paul received Christ, he gained an entirely new perspective on what it means to reign. Instead of his valued Roman citizenship he now claimed, *our citizenship, however, is in heaven, and it is from there that we eagerly wait for a Savior, the Lord Jesus, the Messiah* (Philippians 3:20 ISV). And instead of taking pride in his accomplishments and education, Paul considered *everything else is worthless when compared with the infinite value of knowing Christ Jesus my Lord. For his sake I have discarded everything else, counting it all as garbage, so that I could gain Christ* (Philippians 3:8 NLT). When we exchange the identity we've built for ourselves, for an identity in Christ—we reign!

Spiritual Discipline in Action

Karla always struggled with finding her identity in her success, whether it was academics, sports, friendships, or career. From a young age Karla was very performance oriented and longed to be someone significant. But all too often she confused excellence with perfection. She knew God loved her, she knew her family loved her, but at the core of her being she had a lingering question: "Am I really good enough?"

Rather than let the love of Jesus and who she was in Christ define her, Karla was easily affected by good or bad days. Success, status, and looking the part held her captive. "If I could look good, I could hide that I didn't feel like I was good enough for God or anyone," said Karla.

Senior year of high school, Karla received a scholarship to play college softball at a Division 1 school. "This was a big deal, I had arrived and felt worthy," Karla said. However, things quickly changed when Karla arrived at school.

She was in a whole new environment, a new team, and new location, far from everything she had ever known. Shortly after she left for school, she also found out her dad was sick with cancer. Karla's world was rocked. "My solid foundation of family was being rocked. I tried to put my faith in the Lord but I found myself getting more and more homesick, more and more lost. I felt out of control. So I tried to figure out what I could control. I knew that if I played better, performed better, I would feel good."

Karla trained harder, practiced harder, ran more, and lifted more. But the more she did, the worse it got. "Every time I tried to find my significance in my success, there was no reward. The Lord was stripping me from my own measure of significance and asking me to run to him."

Karla's rock bottom drove her to her knees. But it didn't happen right away. It was a process. It was a battle of control. "Now I can live in His truth, free and alive because God created me as me and I am significant in Him as His child," Karla exclaims.

That summer, Karla was lead to join a softball mission trip in China. She didn't compete. She led clinics for young Chinese girls to teach them how to play softball and share the love of Jesus. "That experience reminded me that God has given me gifts and abilities to use for Him. And in their proper place, my gifts and talents are valuable, not for myself, but for the kingdom. And I can find significance in bringing the Lord glory through how He has wired me. My eyes were opened that summer."

From that point on, Karla had a renewed perspective on the sport of softball. It wasn't about her. It wasn't for her glory. It is all for the Lord. "When I chose to live in that truth, God opened doors that looked different from things I would have chosen for myself. God had plans for me. And I had to choose Him so I could choose abundance in something greater than myself. God can do more than we ask or imagine." Karla learned what it meant to reign in her true identity. The spiritual discipline of *detachment* calls us to remove the very things that taint our true identity in Christ. Whether it is thoughts, motives, failure, or success, our identity should be rooted in Christ alone.

Discipline—*Detachment*
Purpose: To develop and grow in a spirit that trusts and leans upon God solely. To detach or remove idolatrous ideas or motives I associate with, for an identity and attachment to God alone.

Reflection Questions
1. Paul relied heavily on his heritage, citizenship, and education as a source of pride and identity. List any labels or successes you may currently associate with as a source of pride.

2. How would you describe yourself without the above labels? Take a few minutes to describe yourself without using any of the above labels and without listing any of your accomplishments.

3. How has your self-worth been associated with success and labels?

4. What areas of sin are you currently attached? Take a few minutes to list and confess areas of sin from which you need to detach.

Take 20 minutes to read Matthew 16:24-25 and reflect upon what it means and looks like in your life to detach from the things that are not of God.

Then Jesus said to his disciples, "Whoever wants to be my disciple must deny themselves and take up their cross and follow me. For whoever wants to save their life will lose it, but whoever loses their life for me will find it
(Matthew 16:24-25).

Chapter Overview

1. The inheritance to Reign is at the core our purpose on earth and is at the core of the image and likeness in which we were created.
2. God calls us a "chosen people" and His "special possession.

3. Like Jesus, the Holy Spirit also anoints believers in Christ. This anointing empowers us in many ways like Jesus.

4. The anointing of The Holy Spirit reveals to us the truth of who Christ is and the truth of who we are in Christ.

5. We reign with Christ! We win with Christ! We are blessed by the Father, redeemed by Christ, and anointed by the Holy Spirit.

6. We reign in holiness, when we reign over the things that are not of Christ. We reign in holiness when we reign over the things that do not bring God glory, that do not reflect His image correctly.

7. We reign in the freedom of our salvation as a new creation in Christ.

8. When we exchange the identity we've built for ourselves, for an identity in Christ . . .. We Reign!

Related Scriptures

- Genesis 1:26–31
- 2 Timothy 2:12
- 1 Corinthians 6:3
- Romans 6:14
- 1 John 2:27

CHAPTER 6

Reign as a Disciple

*Jesus said, "If you hold to my teaching, you are really
my disciples. Then you will know the truth, and
the truth will set you free"*
(John 8:31-32).

As a Pharisee, Paul found his identity in cultural pride and privilege. He studied under the great master teacher Gamaliel, and appeared to have all the answers. Paul's zeal hid his spiritual blindness and the reality of his hardened heart. He spread a gospel of hate, a gospel that rejected Christ and persecuted His followers. However, Paul encountered Christ and learned very quickly that he had attached his identity to the wrong things. When Paul encountered Christ, he began to reign in life. When Paul attached himself to "the perfect teacher," we have in Christ, Paul reigned as a disciple. In this chapter we will study what it means to reign as a disciple.

What Is a Disciple?

A disciple (*mathētēs* in the Greek) is a student, learner, apprentice, or committed follower. Jesus had a special circle of 12 men whom He called His disciples. Jesus called them individually to learn under His training and eventually carry the gospel to world. He equipped them to make new disciples; in fact He commissioned them to make everyone a disciple (Matthew 28:18-20). Today, the name *disciple* is designated to all Christians that follow Christ.

Rob Bell created a short film entitled "Dust" which explains the significance of discipleship in the historical context of the Bible. In those days, children completed a series of synagogue school trainings, learning and memorizing the Torah, the Mishnah, and the Talmud. When a student completed the series, they would apply to study under a Rabbi (Master of Torah), a Jewish scholar and religious leader. If a Rabbi saw potential in a young student, or thought he could one day "do what he does," the Rabbi would reply; "Follow me." If the Rabbi did not believe the young student had the potential to be like him, or do what he does, the Rabbi would reject him and the student would return to his family trade.

Rob Bell entitles his short film "Dust" because of a familiar Jewish saying, "May you be covered by the dust of your Rabbi." As a disciple follows closely behind their Rabbi, following his every move, training in his ways, striving to be like him, and to one day do what he does; a disciple is covered by the trails of dust of his Rabbi. Could you imagine following so closely behind Christ that the dust of His feet covered you? That we trained and followed behind Christ so closely to become like Him, and live like Him? This is what being a disciple truly means.

The awesome thing about being Jesus' disciple is that He pursues us. Jewish disciples applied to train under a Rabbi, and also faced fear of rejection. The Rabbi only wanted the best of the best to study under him. Jesus, on the other hand, pursues His disciples and asks them to take up their cross and follow Him. In the eyes of Christ, we have potential to do what He does and live in His ways. In the eyes of Christ, we are the best of the best!

Reflection Questions
1. Jesus pursued workingmen to be His original 12 disciples. The synagogue schools and Rabbis rejected

these men, however, Jesus single handedly chose them. What does this say about Jesus' character? How does it feel to be selected by Jesus?

2. Jesus trained His 12 to go and make disciples; we have all heard the gospel of Christ because of their efforts. How did you first learn about Christ? Is there a particular person that shared or explained the gospel to you?

3. All of us owe our salvation to those who continue to spread the good news of Christ. Take a moment to pray and thank God for those who have shared Christ with us.

My Sunday School Teacher

Ms. Bell. What can I say about Ms. Bell? She was my outspoken, fast-talking, energetic Sunday school teacher. Ms. Bell spoke her mind, but always spoke the truth "in love." Ms. Bell helped me take my faith to the next level by teaching me how to pray. I remember being eight years old and sitting in her class on the second floor of the church nursery. We began a lesson on how to pray, and this lesson transformed my life forever. Prior to this lesson, I prayed before meals and when I wanted God to move my parents to give me what I wanted; but that was the extent of my prayer life.

This particular Sunday, we took time to look at the "Lord's Prayer," and this moment showed me how my prayer life was a monolog and not a conversation with God. I never prayed for others, and I always got straight to the point—what I wanted and needed from God. We will take a look at the principles I learned about prayer in the following sections, now we will look at the perfect teacher we have in Jesus.

The Perfect Teacher

I had Ms. Bell and Paul had Gamaliel, but we reign as a disciple because we have a perfect teacher in Christ. In Christ we have a teacher who knows all truth because His is truth. In Christ we have a teacher who defines love because He is love. In Christ we have a teacher that defines sacrifice to the point of death. Finally in Christ, we have a teacher that not only wants us to actively grow and mature as students, but also to grow as a friend. True discipleship leads to a relationship with Christ.

To add to your titles of Image Bearers, Heirs, Royalty, and Disciple, Christ wants to call you a friend. Christ died so our relationship with Him could be restored. Christ also died so those who believe in Him could dwell in His Presence. Christ promises to be with us to end of the age (Matthew 28:20), and as a disciple we learn to recognize and cherish His presence.

How to Build a Relationship With God?

Building a relationship with God may seem very mysterious. God is not physically here and we can't touch him or receive an immediate response. It may even feel impossible to evaluate and determine where you stand in your relationship with God. However, God has created us for relationship and building a relationship with Him is not any different from building a relationship with one another.

We get to know God by making time for Him. We communicate with God through prayer and we get to know Him through the Bible. We will take a closer look at communicating with God through prayer and hearing His voice through Scripture.

Prayer

Prayer is communication with God. Through prayer we can express our feelings, attitudes, and requests to God. We often overload our prayers with requests, but prayer allows us constant fellowship and connection to God. Prayer is imperative to building a relationship with God and God desires this fellowship. God desires a relationship with us so much that He commands us to pray.

Prayer Is Commanded

He then told them a parable on the need for them to pray always and not become discouraged (Luke 18:1 HCSB).

Jesus uses a parable of a persistent widow to teach a powerful lesson about prayer. This widow insistently pursued a judge for justice against her adversary. However, the judge had no fear of God or respect for men, and became annoyed with her persistence. The widow continued to plead her case until the judge gave in. The judge admits:

Even though I don't fear God or respect man, yet because this widow keeps pestering me, I will give her justice, so she doesn't wear me out by her persistent coming (Luke 18:4-5 HCSB).

Jesus' Lesson

Listen to what the unjust judge says. Will not God grant justice to His elect who cry out to Him day and night? Will He delay to help them? I tell you that He will swiftly grant them justice. Nevertheless, when the Son of Man comes, will He find that faith on earth? (Luke 18:6-8 HCSB).

Jesus explains that His disciples must commit themselves to prayer. We must pray faithfully and without ceasing, never giving up on the hope of God's justice. We must also pray continuously with the faith that our prayers will be answered. If ungodly men can grant our requests, how much more will our loving God grant the desires and needs of our heart? In steps towards building our relationship with God, we must pursue Him in prayer. We must make time to meet with Him and share our hearts. We must also trust that God hears and answers our prayers.

Prayer Is Learned

If you feel a bit discouraged by the command to pray because you think you do not pray well or eloquently; the fact that prayer is learned may give you a bit of hope! The initial twelve disciples also had questions about prayer. Jesus took time to show them how to pray. Jesus explains that prayer is intimate and between you and God. He explains that many try to be eloquent with words and babble to prove their religious devotion, yet God simply wants fellowship with you. Jesus models prayer in this way:

Our Father which art in heaven, Hallowed be thy name. Thy kingdom come, Thy will be done in earth, as it is in heaven. Give us this day our daily bread. And forgive us our debts, as we forgive our debtors. And lead us not into temptation, but deliver us from evil: For thine is the kingdom, and the power, and the glory, forever. Amen (Matthew 6:9-13 KJV).

The Lord's Prayer teaches us to:

1. Acknowledge and exalt God (v. 9)

2. Pray and desire for the will of God to be accomplished (v.10)

3. Ask for God to provide for your needs (v.11)

4. Confess sin and ask for forgiveness (v.12)

5. Pray for power over sin and power to forgive (v.12-13)

The Lord's Prayer demonstrates that God should be honored in prayer, but it also shows God's concern for physical and spiritual needs. *"Give us this day, our daily bread"* and *"lead us not into temptation"* displays that we should seek God for all things. From spiritual to personal needs, God wants to hear it all. Paul urged us not to *worry about anything; instead, pray about everything. Tell God what you need, and thank him for all he has done* (Philippians 4:6, NLT).

Prayer Is Empowered

As we have learned more of God's character, we trust that God will not command something of us without bestowing upon us power for success. God expects us to pray, but also He empowers our prayers. Our prayers are empowered even when we don't know what to say or what to pray for. Our efforts in prayer are empowered by the Holy Spirit.

The Spirit helps us in our weakness. We do not know what we ought to pray for, but the Spirit himself intercedes for us through wordless groans. And he who

*searches our hearts knows the mind of the Spirit, be-
cause the Spirit intercedes for God's people in accord-
ance with the will of God (Romans 8:26-27).*

The Spirit searches our hearts and prays to the Father
on our behalf. We aren't expected to have all the right words
to say, but we are expected to meet the Father through prayer.
God honors the time we spend in prayer and gives us a little
help to be successful in our prayers. We have the Holy Spirit
who intercedes for us and Christ who mediates and bridges
the gap between the Father and us. Because of what Christ
has done we may approach God's throne boldly, and our prayers are heard.

Finally, God empowers our prayers because He
wants us to be powerful and effective. God wants us to win;
God wants us to reign. Apart from God we can do nothing,
but prayer puts us in the position to abide in Him. Read what
Christ says about the praying disciple:

*If you remain in Me and My words remain in you, ask
whatever you want and it will be done for you. My Father
is glorified by this: that you produce much fruit and
prove to be My disciples (John 15:7-8 HCSB).*

Reflection Questions

1. How often do you pray? What tends to be the focus
   of your prayers?

2. If prayer leads to a relationship with God, how often
   should we pray? What can you do to increase and improve our prayer routine?

3. James 5:16 says, *The prayers of the righteous are powerful and effective.* What makes prayer "powerful and effective"? How can we become more effective in our prayers?

The Bible

Communication is essential to a lasting relationship. We communicate with God through prayer, however our communication is not one-sided. God answers every prayer and speaks primarily through His Word. "Scripture is God's primary means of special revelation, because it provides a permanent record of what God intends for humans to know about Him, His works, and His plan."[7] God's Word is trustworthy and is a guide to know our God intimately, but also there are many rewards.

A Command and A Promise

This book of instruction must not depart from your mouth; you are to recite it day and night so that you may carefully observe everything written in it. For then you will prosper and succeed in whatever you do (Joshua 1:8 HCSB).

What is God's command?

What is God's Promise?

while he was still speaking, a rooster crowed (Luke 22:56b-60 HCSB).

Once the rooster crowed, Peter remembered what Jesus had predicted. Peter ran away weeping for what he had done. The crowed went on to mock and beat Jesus as He faced trial. Jesus was eventually sentenced to death for refusing to deny that He was the Son of God. This was His mission, to die for the sins of the world, and to be a once and for all sacrifice for sin. However, Christ's death left His disciples distressed and confused about the will of the Father.

Peter and the disciples soon learned that Jesus defeated death and rose from the dead on the third day. We know the good news of Jesus' resurrection and what that means for our relationship with God; however Peter also needed to learn this powerful lesson. When Jesus revealed Himself to the disciples, He was intentional with His encounter with Peter.

When they had eaten breakfast, Jesus asked Simon Peter, "Simon, son of John, do you love Me more than these?" "Yes, Lord," he said to Him, "You know that I love You." "Feed My lambs," He told him. A second time He asked him, "Simon, son of John, do you love Me?" "Yes, Lord," he said to Him, "You know that I love You." "Shepherd My sheep," He told him. He asked him the third time, "Simon, son of John, do you love Me?" Peter was grieved that He asked him the third time, "Do you love Me?" He said, "Lord, You know everything! You know that I love You." "Feed My sheep," Jesus said... "Follow Me" (John 21:15-19 HCSB).

Jesus restores Peter three times, showing Peter that he was forgiven for the three times he denied Jesus. In each of Jesus' responses, He gives Peter an opportunity to pledge his love, but also commissions Peter to put that love into action. Peter goes on to be a hero of our faith and a pillar of the

Christian church. Peter's story shows us how we need to follow Jesus no matter the circumstance; but also it shows us the forgiveness of God. Like Peter, our relationship with Christ is on good terms. Let's continue to nourish our relationship with God and reign in our position as His friend.

Spiritual Discipline in Action

My older sister Tuccoa is one of my best friends in the world. I look up to her in so many ways. She was the first in our family to graduate college and finish her Masters. She was the first to leave the city and live on her own. She is the real deal! She was like a second mom growing up, and for some reason, my parents trusted her to have those tough coming of age conversations with me. In many ways I used Tuccoa's life as a springboard and example of what to do and not to do. I praise God for a big sister who would lead the way for me, to go through life's bumps and bruises to spare me the heartache. I learned very early how wise people learn from the mistakes of others, and God used Tuccoa as a shield in many ways.

As I grew in ministry Tuccoa would call me her "Sister Reverend Ty Ty," and would always ask me various theological questions. Over the years I would hear a theme in her language. The phrase "losing my salvation" continued to come up. Somewhere along her walk with Christ, she was either taught or believed she could lose her salvation. Like God holds a tally of the good and bad things we do. If we wind up on the wrong side of this "good deed" count we may lose salvation. Could you imagine living with this amount of uncertainty? Would the good news of the gospel really be good news, or just false hope? We would consistently use Scriptures to justify our security and seal in Christ. However, I didn't know if Tuccoa was completely persuaded that she was secure in Christ, until I read one of her social media posts. My sister was preaching to masses and boldly says:

"Our pastor said something Sunday that makes this point—you can know God (books) and not KNOW God (His nature). I know God and I'm working daily to grow more intimate and closer to Him. THAT'S what Christianity is—a personal relationship with Jesus who you accept and believe is the Son of God, who lived a perfect and sinless 33.5 yrs. on this earth and who CHOSE to die for our sins. Who gives His salvation freely, for there is not a single thing we can do to lose it because there is absolutely NOTHING we can do to earn it!"

Yes, she gets it! Salvation is a free gift from God, and sometimes we need to remind ourselves of this precious gift. When we get caught up in earning salvation or earning the love of God, we need to remind ourselves of the love of Christ. The spiritual discipline of *praying Scripture* will help to remind us how our relationship with God is on good terms because of the sacrifice of Christ.

Discipline—*Praying Scripture*
Purpose: To allow God to direct and shape your prayer life through His Word, the Bible. This opens the heart to God's truth through psalms, hymns, promises, prayers, and testimonies found in Scriptures. Praying Scripture allows you to speak the truth of God's Word over your life and positions you to pray the will of God.

Take 20 Min to Pray the Scriptures
Allow God to guide your prayer through praying the following verses over your life and making it personal. Insert your name and claim the promises of God.

For Example: "If God is for (insert name), who can be against (Insert name)?"

Romans 8: 31-35, 37

What, then, shall we say in response to these things? If God is for us, who can be against us? He who did not spare his own Son, but gave him up for us all—how will he not also, along with him, graciously give us all things?

Who will bring any charge against those whom God has chosen? It is God who justifies. Who then is the one who condemns? No one. Christ Jesus who died—more than that, who was raised to life—is at the right hand of God and is also interceding for us.

Who shall separate us from the love of Christ? Shall trouble or hardship or persecution or famine or nakedness or danger or sword?

No, in all these things we are more than conquerors through him who loved us.

Be sure to thank God for what He says about you and has done for you. If you have a hard time believing that you are "More than a Conquer," pray for God to help your unbelief. If there are more verses you have grown to love, pray them over your life. Praying Scripture is a sure way to pray the will of God and become familiar with the voice of God.

Chapter Overview

1. A disciple (*mathētēs* in the Greek) is a student, learner, or committed follower.

2. We reign as a disciple of Christ because we have a perfect teacher in Christ. In Christ we have a teacher who knows all truth because His is truth. In Christ we have a teacher who defines loves, because He is love.

3. God has created us for relationship and building a relationship with Him is not any different from building a relationship with one another. We communicate with God through prayer and we get to know Him through the Bible.

4. Prayer is communication with God. Through prayer we can express our feelings, attitudes, and requests to God.

5. Prayer is empowered by God. The Spirit searches our hearts and prays to the Father on our behalf.

6. God Communicates primarily through Scripture.

7. Scripture is God-breathed and reveals the voice of God. Knowing God's voice helps us to distinguish what God is truly saying to us.

Related Scriptures

- Psalm 34:15
- John 14:14
- Ephesians 6:18
- James 5:16
- 1 John 5:15
- 2 Timothy 3:16

CHAPTER 7

Reign Through Obedience

*For it is not those who hear the law who are righteous in God's
sight, but it is those who obey the law who will
be declared righteous*
(Romans 2:13).

uring Jesus' earthly ministry He encountered many
who were in need of physical and spiritual healing,
as well as those who sought to go deeper in their
faith. While on a journey to Jerusalem, Jesus encountered a rich ruler, who ran to Him and knelt at His feet
with an urgent question. The young rich ruler exclaimed,
"Good Teacher, what must I do to inherit eternal life?" This
young man, a possible leader of a synagogue, would not miss
an opportunity to have Jesus answer his pressing question. He
ran with urgency, and knelt at Jesus' feet with his plea. However, Jesus knowing the man's heart replies:

> *You know the commandments: Do not murder; do not
> commit adultery; do not steal; do not bear false witness;
> do not defraud; honor your father and mother (Mark
> 10:19 HCSB)*

Jesus cites five of the Ten Commandments that relate to a person's relationship and attitude towards others. Jesus omits the first commandment (Thou shall have no other gods before me) and the tenth command, (Thou shall not covet) and we will soon see why. The young man responds in verse 20, *"Teacher I have kept all these from my youth."* Jesus looks to the young man with love and compassion, as He reveals the true condition of the young man's heart.

"You lack one thing: Go, sell all you have and give to the poor, and you will have treasure in heaven. Then come, follow Me" (Mark 10:21b HCSB).

The young ruler left the feet of Jesus in despair. He had many possessions and the thought of parting with he's riches was devastating. However, the emphasis of Jesus' question was not in "sell all of your possessions," but on "follow me." Jesus used the command "sell all you have" to prove that wealth was the god over the young ruler's life. Jesus' command was simply to give full allegiance to God. The young ruler could only focus on losing his wealth and dismissed the invitation to become a true disciple. The young man did not suffer from an issue of disobedience, but of lordship. The ultimate command of the Kingdom of God is not to religiously follow rules, but to pledge allegiance to Jesus and allow Him to be Lord over your life.

Jesus' Response: *You lack one thing*

The young ruler struggled with selling his possessions. His wealth was a stumbling block, which prevented him from becoming a true disciple of Christ. Jesus offered him an opportunity to follow Him, and learn from Him within His special group. Jesus offered the same invitation to this young ruler; *follow me* that He offered to the other exclusive 12. The possessions of this unnamed ruler where in the way of true discipleship; if Jesus were to tell you: *You lack one thing*, what would that one thing be?

Take a few moments to consider what's holding you back from absolute allegiance to Jesus. As you ponder this question, this chapter will help us discover how we reign through obedience.

Lordship

The rich ruler struggled with lordship. He refused to allow Jesus to be his priority and master over his life. The young man sought the "Great Teacher," but not the "Great Commander" who would require a sacrifice through obedience. Jesus requires obedience to the point of losing everything. Jesus was a "great teacher" in name to the young ruler, but not the ultimate authority, which true discipleship requires.

Lordship is authority or submission given to one who is a master or one who calls the shots in your life. Jesus is called "Lord" 747 times in the New Testament. There is biblical emphasis on the Lordship of Christ for an important reason. If you want to have Jesus as Savior, He must also be Lord. We must be willing to submit our life completely to the will of God, to voluntarily yield to Christ as the ultimate authority over our life.

Call me Lord, Lord

In contrast to the young ruler, there was a tax collector named Zacchaeus who also desired to restore his life to God. Zacchaeus was also rich, but from his notorious position as a tax collector. The tax collectors of that time became rich from exploiting families through inflated taxes. Zacchaeus' ill-gotten wealth is placed in stark contrast to the young ruler, for Zacchaeus was viewed outwardly as a sinner, while the young ruler was seen as one who obeyed the commandments from youth.

Similarly to the unnamed ruler, Zacchaeus was desperate to see Jesus. As Jesus entered the city of Jericho, Zacchaeus climbed a sycamore tree to ensure he saw Jesus. Zacchaeus was short in stature and did whatever it took to put himself in position to see Him. When Jesus passed by the tree, Jesus looked up and said *"Zacchaeus, hurry and come down because today I must stay at your house"* (Luke 19:5 HCSB). Zacchaeus came down quickly from the tree to greet Jesus. Many in the crowd complained about Jesus lodging with a sinner. However, here's Zacchaeus' response:

> *Look, I'll give half of my possessions to the poor, Lord! And if I have extorted anything from anyone, I'll pay back four times as much!" (Luke 19:8 HCSB).*

Jesus' Response

> *"Today salvation has come to this house," Jesus told him, "because he too is a son of Abraham. For the Son of Man has come to seek and to save the lost (Luke 19:9-10 HCSB).*

Appearance vs. Heart

The young rich ruler appeared to be right with God. He followed the commandments and served his people. On the other hand, Zacchaeus was viewed as a notorious sinner who exploited his people. Both faced sin rooted in their riches but only one was willing to lose his riches to be restored to God. Zacchaeus was willing to give his possessions to the poor and repay the money he had extorted. Jesus had not asked Zacchaeus to sell his possessions, but Zacchaeus knew it was the right thing to do. Zacchaeus immediately did what the rich ruler refused to do, and he was rewarded for this act of obedience.

If Jesus made arrangements to lodge with the young rich ruler, the crowd would not have objected. However, Jesus was ridiculed for lodging with Zacchaeus, and he was the one who surrendered his riches. Zacchaeus was willing to allow Jesus, not money, to be Lord over his life. The Bible warns us against being Christians in title and not in our hearts:

Not everyone who says to me, 'Lord, Lord,' will enter the kingdom of heaven, but only the one who does the will of my Father who is in heaven. Many will say to me on that day, 'Lord, Lord, did we not prophesy in your name and in your name drive out demons and in your name perform many miracles?' Then I will tell them plainly, 'I never knew you. Away from me, you evildoers!' (Matthew 7:21-23).

I Never Knew You

God wants a relationship with you. The example of Matthew chapter 7 shows those that seemingly perform miracles in the name of Lord, but do not pledge allegiance to Him. They appear to be upright and righteous, but they lack one thing: Lordship. The Lordship of Christ is essential to Christian faith because, authentic Lordship leads to obedience. God commands obedience, but the obedience He desires is rooted in relationship with Him.

The Obedience of Jesus

Jesus perfectly obeyed the will of the Father to the point of death. Many recognize the result of Christ's sacrifice, eternal life; yet many need to be reminded of the depth of anguish Jesus faced. Jesus pleads with the Father, requesting another way to save mankind; that the cup of physical and spiritual sufferings be removed. "*My Father! If it is possible. Let this cup pass from Me. Yet not as I will, but as You will*" (Matthew 26:39b). Jesus knew that He would be betrayed, humiliated, and suffer a public death. Anguish and stress took over His mind and spirit until He began to sweat blood. Medical literature notes the condition of "sweating blood"; it is rare but does occur in humans. The condition is commonly known as hematidrosis, resulting from the rupture of sweat glands, mixing one's blood with perspiration. Hematidrosis is caused by great emotional distress, acute fear, and extreme mental contemplation.

Even before His physical death, Jesus suffered beyond what we can imagine. The thought of sin and its deadly effects, as well as being separated from the Father inflicted pain upon Jesus beyond comprehension. Jesus would soon take on the sin of the world, and become sin. He took on the punishment of the world, so we may be forgiven. He was separated from the Father, so we may be reconciled and restored to the Father. Nevertheless, Jesus surrendered to the will of the Father because of His love for us. Love motivated Jesus and love is the only proper motive for obedience. Fear and force may result in obedience temporarily, but love moves the heart to true change.

Empowered to Obey

God commands us to obey because He created us to be holy and set apart. The Bible reminds us that just *as he who called you is holy, you also be holy in all your conduct* (1 Peter 1:15 ESV). We were created to reflect His holy image, and obedience to His commands is necessary to do so. Since our calling and purpose is to live righteous lives, God empowers us to be successful in obedience to His Word. Like any other command of God, He never sets us up to fail. God always provides a way for His people to accomplish His will. So how does God empower us to have victory over sin? We are empowered by love and the Holy Spirit to obey God.

Empowered by Love
If you love Me, you will keep My commands
(John 14:15 HCSB).

*The one who has My commands and keeps them is the one
who loves Me. And the one who loves Me will be loved by
My Father. I also will love him and will reveal Myself to him*
(John 14:21 HCSB).

Empowered by the Holy Spirit
*But the Helper, the Holy Spirit, whom the Father will send
in my name, he will teach you all things and bring to your remembrance all that I have said to you* (John 14:26 ESV).

*For John baptized with water, but you will be baptized with
the Holy Spirit not many days from now... But you will receive power when the Holy Spirit has come on you.*
(Acts 1:5, 8a HCSB)

When we accept Jesus as Savior, we receive the Holy
Spirit. The Holy Spirit is our Helper who not only helps us to
pray but also enables us to obey God. The Holy Spirit empowers us to accomplish the will of God by moving our hearts
to complete surrender to God. Our hearts are moved by love
and relationship with God. Our hearts are moved by the constant reminder of how and why we were created; and knowing
who we are in Christ leads to obedience.

Doers of the Word

*But be doers of the word and not hearers only, deceiving
yourselves. Because if anyone is a hearer of the word
and not a doer, he is like a man looking at his own face
in a mirror. For he looks at himself, goes away, and immediately forgets what kind of man he was. But the one
who looks intently into the perfect law of freedom and*

perseveres in it, and is not a forgetful hearer but one who does good works—this person will be blessed in what he does (James 1:22-25 HCSB).

James, the brother of Jesus, concerns his entire book of the Bible on *Christianity in Action*. James is concerned with the Christian that does not act like a Christian. In the verses above, James simply encourages the reader not only to hear the Word of God, but also to put those words into action. James gives an example of one who does not put the Word of God in action. He depicts the person as one who looks in a mirror, walks away and *immediately forgets what kind of man he was.*

When we disobey God, we forget who we are. We forget we are His Image Bearers, created to reflect His image to the world. We forget we are heiresses representing our Father's business. We forget we are filled and empowered by the Holy Spirit to defeat sin and death. Finally, we forget the sacrifice of Christ and the sufferings He endured to save us from sin. However, when we are doers of the Word of God, we function in our purpose and the Image in which we were created. Obeying the commands of God honors Him, and the Bible promises that we are blessed when we obey.

Repentance

Finally, true Lordship will result in obedience that leads to repentance. Mature disciples have transformed minds, which results in an inward change of attitudes and perspectives; but also an outward change in actions. Authentic discipleship leads to repentance because repentance requires faith and obedience. Repentance in the Hebrew is *Šîbâ/Šûb* meaning, turning, restoration, or to return. Repentance in the Greek New Testament is *metanoia/ metanoeō* meaning, a change in mind or to change one's mind. Let's take a moment to discover how we reign in repentance.

The author of the book of Hebrews urges believers in Christ to mature in their faith and move on to weightier matters concerning discipleship. The author uses the analogy of a child needing milk, while an adult matures to consume solid foods. Likewise, mature Disciples of Christ should mature to the solid, weightier ideals of our faith. One of the weightier teachings of our faith is repentance. Repentance involves turning away from sin and turning to a life of righteousness with God. Repentance also involves faith, trusting that God will bless and empower us to live righteous lives. Both Paul and Zacchaeus are great examples of godly repentance from sin. Both had a change in heart that led to restoration with Christ. Paul and Zacchaeus also experienced godly sorrow that leads to remorse and regret of their sinful lifestyles. Godly sorrow is the only lasting motive for repentance.

Godly sorrow brings repentance that leads to salvation and leaves no regret, but worldly sorrow brings death (2 Cor. 7:10).

Paul explains how godly sorrow results in repentance that leads to salvation, while in contrast worldly sorrow leads to death. Worldly sorrow leads to death because worldly sorrow is more concerned about being caught, or what sin does to one's reputation. Worldly sorrow is short lived and does not lead one to turning away from sin and towards God. Similarly, the young rich ruler experienced worldly sorrow that did not lead to repentance; it actually drove him further away from God. On the other hand, godly sorrow leads to repentance because we understand we have sinned against God. Godly sorrow reminds us of who God is, and our desperate condition apart from Him. Godly sorrow allows us to focus on Jesus' invitation to "follow me," and not on His commands that are unfavorable to us.

Repentance is essential to reigning in life because repentance, turning to God and away from sin, keeps us in the presence of God. The Bible teaches us that apart from God we can do nothing (John 15:5), but with God all things are possible (Matthew 19:26). The key to reigning in life as a disciple is to remain in His presence. *I am the vine, you are the branches. The one who remains in Me and I in him produces much fruit, because you can do nothing without Me* (John 15:5 HCSB).

Spiritual Discipline in Action

Discipline—*Submission*
Purpose: To make Jesus the Lord and Master of our lives. Godly submission is to freely give over our will and desires for the will of God.

The word *submit* is one of the most difficult and disliked principles of the Bible. Submitting to God is freeing ourselves from the need to be in charge. We want to call the shots, we believe we know what's best for ourselves; however, we do **not** know what's best for ourselves. The author and creator of all things not only knows how and why He made you, but knows what's best for you.

Take 10 min to answer the following reflection questions:

1. Submitting is obeying the will of God, even when it leads to a seemingly undesirable place (for example, selling all of your possessions). What may God be calling you to do, that currently feels undesirable?

2. The Rich Young Ruler viewed God's command to sell his possessions as undesirable. However, the

young man passed on an opportunity to be a member of Jesus' 12 hand- selected disciples. What does this story show you about the character of God? How does this story help you believe that God rewards obedience?

Read Mark 10: 29-30a and answer the following question:

"I assure you," Jesus said, "there is no one who has left house, brothers or sisters, mother or father, children, or fields because of Me and the gospel, who will not receive 100 times more."

3. Jesus promises to reward those who make sacrifices for their faith in Him. How have you already begun to see the rewards of your faith?

Take 20 min. to pray and thank God for promises. Finally, ask God to empower you to submit to Him and His will, as well as the authority figures God has placed in your life (boss, pastor, teacher, spouse etc.).

Chapter Overview

1. The ultimate command of the Kingdom of God is not to religiously follow rules, but to pledge allegiance to Jesus and allow Him to be Lord over your life.

2. Lordship is authority or submission given to one who is a master or one who call the shots in your life.

3. Jesus is called "Lord" 747 times in the New Testament.

4. The Lordship of Christ is essential to Christian faith because, authentic Lordship leads to obedience. God commands obedience, but the obedience He desires is rooted in relationship with Him.

5. Since our calling and purpose is to live righteous lives, God empowers us to be successful in obedience to His word.

6. We are empowered to obey God by love and the Holy Spirit.

7. When we disobey God, we forget who we are. We forget that we are His Image Bearers, created to reflect His image to the world.

8. Paul explains that godly sorrow results in repentance that leads to salvation, while in contrast worldly sorrow leads to death.

Related Scriptures

- Jeremiah 11:4
- John 14:15
- 1 John 5:2
- 2 Timothy 2:25-26
- 1 Corinthians 15:34

CHAPTER 8

Reign in Faith

*Keeping our eyes on Jesus, the source
and perfecter of our faith*
(Hebrew 12:2 HCSB).

Keeping our eyes on Jesus . . . but what if we don't see Him?" exclaimed Megan. "What if our life and reality we live each day is contrary to the principles of Jesus. The Bible teaches to submit to Jesus as Lord, but don't we reign when we have control?" Megan was feisty and brought another perspective to the group. She didn't just go with the crowd, but asked tough questions. Megan had a mind of her own, and I loved this about her. Many of us may also have these tough questions about faith, but may keep them to ourselves. Faith is not mysterious, but in many ways is contrary to the world. Faith is the basis of Christianity. This is why the Bible calls us to *work out your salvation with fear and trembling*, because it is a big deal! This passage doesn't just shake us up, but it confirms what faith does within us: *for it is God who works in you to will and to act in order to fulfill his good purpose* (Philippians 2:12-13). Faith allows God to work in and through us!

The last chapter discussed how we reign in repentance, because repentance is motivated by faith. We believe turning to Jesus will result in forgiveness and salvation. We reign through repentance because we turn to Jesus; we reign in faith because it allows us to walk with God and remain in His presence. In this chapter we will explore the type of faith all Disciples of Christ should strive for, and learn what it means to reign in faith.

What Is Faith?

Faith is belief, trust, or confidence in a person or idea. We all display some level faith every day. For example we believe the chair we seat on will support us or the sun will eventually shine after a storm. We even believe in what we do not see, for example air or gravity. Without faith, we would live a life full of uncertainties that would wreck our lives. Could you imagine living uncertain of literally every step you took? Living unsure that the ground you stand on can support you, or being unsure your water is secure in its glass. Even atheists display faith in these natural orders of the world; this is called natural faith. However, the faith that causes us to reign in life and in our purpose requires a deeper type of faith.

Types of Faith

The Bible describes at least three types of faith, which in fact aren't faith at all: head faith, "see it" faith, and dead faith. First, *head faith* is a faith that is intellectual and rooted in knowledge of facts. Head faith never stretches the heart beyond what is certain. For example one can say they have faith that God will provide for their mortgage payment, only because they know they have enough in their bank account to cover it. One can also believe in Jesus because of historical facts about Him. In the book of James, James gives a great example of a person with head faith and sarcastically congratulates them.

You say you have faith, for you believe that there is one God. Good for you! Even the demons believe this, and they tremble in terror (James 2:19 NLT).

James compares those with *head faith* to demons. This may seem a bit harsh, but knowing there is a God does not cause one to live for God. Demons know for a fact God is real. Demons believe in God and have seen Him; yet long to destroy His kingdom and His believers. James clearly states head faith is not the faith of a true disciple of Christ.

Next, there's *see it faith*, where one has to see it, to believe it. *See it* faith is similar to *head faith*, but is not satisfied with facts that can't be seen or physically touched. After the resurrection Jesus revealed Himself to over 500 believers. Jesus had defeated death just as He foretold and revealed Himself to His disciples. One of the disciples named Thomas was not present when Jesus met them. The other disciples continued to explain how they had seen the Lord. However, Thomas did not believe them.

Thomas' Response

If I don't see the mark of the nails in His hands, put my finger into the mark of the nails, and put my hand into His side, I will never believe! (John 20:25b HCSB).

Jesus' Response

After eight days His disciples were indoors again, and Thomas was with them. Even though the doors were locked, Jesus came and stood among them. He said, "Peace to you!" Then He said to Thomas, "Put your finger here and observe My hands. Reach out your hand and put it into My side. Don't be an unbeliever, but a believer." Thomas responded to Him, "My Lord and my God!" (John 20:26-28 HCSB).

Jesus eliminates all of Thomas' doubts as He continues to bear the wounds of the cross. However, Jesus also teaches a valuable lesson about faith. Jesus said, *"Because you have seen Me, you have believed. Those who believe without seeing are blessed"* (John 20: 29 HCSB). Jesus is talking about us! Thomas had the opportunity to walk with Christ and learn from Him, but we believe in Christ and resurrection without ever physically seeing Him; for this we are blessed. There are times when we want to see it to believe it, but the Bible teaches us that disciples of Christ will *walk by faith, not by sight* when our senses oppose our faith (2 Corinthians 5:7).

Finally there is *dead faith*, which is faith void of actions. *Dead faith* is all talk and but no walk. The Bible continuously explains how faith should bring about action, and a faith without action is dead. Faith without works is useless and is not a faith that leads to salvation. The Bible even goes on to say if one does not put their faith into action their *religion is useless and he deceives himself* (James 1:26b HCSB). We are not saved by our actions, but our actions should reveal our faith. A dead faith is no faith at all; the faith that God desires is a soul saving faith.

Soul Saving Faith

God desires for us to have soul saving faith. God desires a faith that not only turns to Jesus for salvation, but also walks with Him for the rest of our lives. Jesus explains this type of faith in the *Parable of the Sower*. Jesus taught in parables to use common experiences to teach Kingdom principles. In the Parable of the Sower, Jesus explains soul saving faith through the experience of a farmer.

Jesus explains how a sower went out to sow with the goal to plant seeds that would eventually produce fruit. As the sower began to throw seeds unto the soil, the seeds fell in various locations. Some seeds fell upon the path, amongst rocky soil, thorny soil, and finally on good soil. Here's a quick description of the four soils.

1. **Path**—Hard packed soil, which seeds could not penetrate. Birds ate some of the seeds.

2. **Rocky Soil**—Shallow soil that covered limestone. Some seeds would begin to sprout fairly quickly, but the sun would scorch the growing seed. Because of its lack of deep roots the plants could not grow strong.

3. **Thorny Soil**—Soil filled with thorny weeds. These seeds would grow, but the weeds grew also, eventually stunting the growth of the plant.

4. **Good Soil**—Deeply rooted and fertilized soil that produced strong long lasting fruit.

As Jesus describes the soils, many are unsure of the underlying meaning of the story. Jesus goes on to explain that the seeds are the Word of God and the soils are the conditions of the heart. Just as the condition of soil determines if a seed will bear fruit, the same is considered of the heart. The condition of the heart will determine if one will receive soul saving faith. Here's how Jesus explains the soils further.

> **Path**—*When anyone hears the word about the kingdom and doesn't understand it, the evil one comes and snatches away what was sown in his heart. This is the one sown along the path* (Matthew 13:19 HSCB).

> **Rocky Soil**—*And the one sown on rocky ground—this is one who hears the word and immediately receives it with joy. Yet he has no root in himself, but is short-lived. When pressure or persecution comes because of the word, immediately he stumbles* (Matthew 13:20-21 HSCB).

Thorny Soil—*Now the one sown among the thorns—this is one who hears the word, but the worries of this age and the seduction of wealth choke the word, and it becomes unfruitful* (Matthew 13:22 HSCB).

Good Soil—*But the one sown on the good ground—this is one who hears and understands the word, who does bear fruit and yields: some 100, some 60, some 30 times what was sown* (Matthew 13:20-21 HSCB).

Reflection Questions

1. Take a moment and read over the soil descriptions and Jesus' explanation of each. Which of the four best describes the condition of your heart? Why?

2. In another parable, Jesus describes the Father as a gardener who prunes or cuts every branch that does not produce fruit (John 15). If the Father were to prune unfruitful areas in your life, what would those areas be? And why?

3. What spiritual fertilizers would help improve the condition of your spiritual soil?

The Fruit of Faith

Soul saving faith is faith rooted in good soil. This soil allows the seed of faith to produce fruit. Fruit that identifies us as believers and fruit that is connected to the one true vine—Christ. Jesus explains in a parable about entering the Kingdom of Heaven, and how His true disciples will be recognized by their fruit. Soul saving faith will produce obedience, forgiveness, peace, and eternal security; soul saving faith also produces power to overcome challenges. Here are three seeds of faith that grew into life changing testimonies.

Mountain Moving Faith

There was a man who came to Jesus on behalf of his son. His son suffered from seizures and would lose control of his body. There were times when he would fall into water or even fire. The men knelt at the feet of Jesus and pleaded for healing for his son. The disciples were unable to heal the young boy and here is Jesus' response.

> Jesus replied, "You unbelieving and rebellious generation! How long will I be with you? How long must I put up with you? Bring him here to Me." Then Jesus rebuked the demon, and it came out of him, and from that moment the boy was healed (Matthew 17: 17-18 HSCB).

Jesus is clearly upset with the lack of faith His disciples displayed. The people looked to them as examples of faith and they lacked faith themselves. The disciples were also disappointed in their inability to heal the young boy. So they approached Jesus privately and asked: why weren't they able to drive out the demon? Jesus replies:

> "Because of your little faith," He told them. "For I assure you: If you have faith the size of a mustard seed, you will tell this mountain, 'Move from here to there,' and it

*will move. Nothing will be impossible for you" (Matthew
17: 20 HCSB).*

Reflection Questions

1. The "mountains" Jesus refers to are life's difficulties.
What hardships or difficulties are playing the role of
mountains in your life?

Jesus explains that with just a "little faith" we can do
the impossible. What have been goals or even circumstances
that seemed impossible to overcome? Learning from the example of the disciples, what should we do when things seem
impossible? Well, here's a solution: Bring it to Jesus. Jesus
commands the disciples to bring the boy to Him. Once they
brought the boy to Jesus, he was healed. Bring your mountains to Jesus. Your way hasn't worked, and like the father
who wasn't content with accepting his circumstance; we must
bring these difficult issues to Jesus and have faith He can
move the mountain on your behalf.

Walking on Water Faith

Jesus placed His disciples in many situations for the
purpose of building their faith. After feeding 5,000 men, not
counting the women and children, with only two fish and five
loaves of bread; Jesus wanted to teach the disciples another
lesson in faith. He commanded the disciples to board the boat
and head to the other side of the lake ahead of Him.

Around three in the morning the boat ran into a storm and rough seas. The disciples were afraid and to add to their terror they saw what appeared to be a ghost walking towards them on the water. As the disciples cried out in fear, Jesus said to them, "Have courage! It is I. Don't be afraid."

Peter's Response

"Lord, if it's You," Peter answered Him, "command me to come to You on the water." "Come!" He said. And climbing out of the boat, Peter started walking on the water and came toward Jesus. But when he saw the strength of the wind, he was afraid. And beginning to sink he cried out, "Lord, save me!" Immediately Jesus reached out His hand, caught hold of him, and said to him, "You of little faith, why did you doubt?" (Matthew 14:27-31 HCSB).

Why did Peter doubt? Peter performed the miracle of walking on water. He stepped out on faith and trusted that he too could walk on water, simply because Jesus said he could. It took courage to step out and trust the command of Jesus, yet Peter began to lose faith in fear of the waves. The courage Peter stirred up to step out of the boat needed to be sustained. If Peter had kept his eyes fixed on Jesus, he would not have noticed the waves; instead Peter would have focused on the miracle of walking on water with Jesus.

Even the disciples needed to mature in faith. Peter learned a valuable lesson to focus on Jesus and not the storm. God may be in the mist of preparing you for something great. A career, a new relationship, or healing may be in the works, so let's keep our eyes on Jesus. Focus on His promises in the midst of a storm. Like Peter, we don't want to miss the miracle by focusing on the storm. Yet, if we do take our eyes off Jesus and began to sink, the good news is that Jesus will always be there to pull us back into the boat.

Healing Faith

The disciple Mark strategically placed two dynamic stories of healing after the teachings of the parables, especially the parable of the sower. The parables distinguish those with false faith and those with soul saving faith. The latter are those who are healed. This story takes place in the hometown of Jesus; it is here where many are faced with the tensions of "faith and fear," and where Jesus teaches His disciples not to be afraid.

First there is Jairus, a synagogue leader, who was determined to find Jesus. Jairus' daughter was 12 years old, and was deathly ill. Jairus' love for his daughter pushed him to fall at the feet of the man whom many of his colleagues (Pharisees, and other Jewish leaders) ridiculed and planned to destroy. However, Jairus was on a mission and knew that Jesus was the only person who could save his daughter.

Jairus' Plea

[Jairus] kept begging Him, "My little daughter is at death's door. Come and lay Your hands on her so she can get well and live." So Jesus went with him, and a large crowd was following and pressing against Him (Mark 5:23-24 HCSB).

While heading to the home of Jairus, the crowd began to follow and press in towards Jesus. Suddenly, Jesus exclaimed, "Who touched me?" The disciples are flustered at the question, because there were so many people around with the opportunity to touch Jesus. So why did Jesus stop and ask this question?

Jesus Is Interrupted

So He was looking around to see who had done this. Then the woman, knowing what had happened to her, came with fear and trembling, fell down before Him, and told Him the whole truth. "Daughter," He said to her, "your faith has made you well. Go in peace and be free from your affliction" (Mark 5: 32-34 HCSB).

Why was a touch from this woman so important to Jesus? Well, this unnamed woman suffered from a condition that caused her to bleed continuously for 12 years. This woman spent all she had going from doctor to doctor to be healed. Unfortunately, her condition became worse. In her social context, women were expected to stay indoors and in isolation during their menstrual cycle. At this time women were considered ceremonially unclean for seven days during this time. For 12 years this woman suffered in isolation, she lived a life similar to that of a leper, who suffered cultic uncleanness and excluded from society. Anything this woman sat on or touched would be considered unclean.

This is why Jesus' acknowledgment of her is so important. First, it shows her faith in Jesus to heal her physically and spiritually. She believed if she could just touch the *hem of His garment*, she would be saved. She risked public scrutiny to step out in bold faith, and Jesus responded with acceptance and healing. Second, Jesus validates her publicly by calling her "daughter," and restores her back to community.

Back to the Story

While He was still speaking, people came from the synagogue leader's house and said, "Your daughter is dead. Why bother the Teacher anymore?" But when Jesus overheard what was said, He told the synagogue leader, "Don't be afraid. Only believe" (Mark 5:35-36 HSCB).

When they entered the home and Jesus informed the people in the house that the girl is merely sleeping, a number of the men in the home begin to laugh. Yes, laugh at Jesus.

Jesus kicks them out of the room where the girl lay, then He brings in Peter, James, John and the girl's parents.

> *Then He took the child by the hand and said to her, "Talitha koum!"(which is translated, "Little girl, I say to you, get up!"). Immediately the girl got up and began to walk. At this they were utterly astounded (Mark 5: 41-42 HCSB).*

A Lesson From the Women Who Touched Jesus

First, let's look at the contrasting differences in these women's lives. An influential father pleads for healing on behalf of his dying daughter, while the other is forced to approach Jesus from behind and in secret. One is 12 years old, while the other suffers with an issue of blood for 12 years. Yet, they are more similar than they appear.

Both women are nameless, one identified by her father and the other by her condition. Both women are rendered unclean; the young woman as a corpse and the woman's issue of blood makes her unclean. These stories bring out the issue of ritual cleanness and uncleanness. Yet, Jesus never hesitates to touch and heal them.

Teachable Moments
1. Make God your first choice

- Jairus tried all He could to save his daughter, but when he heard Jesus was in town he gave Him a try.

- The woman spent all that she had to trying to find a cure for her illness, yet Jesus was the only person who could heal her.

2. Jesus honors our faith, even when its small

- Jesus honors the faith of a woman who believes she can be healed by simply touching His robe. With just a little faith can accomplish so much with Christ.

3. *God is approachable*

- Fear and faith led the woman to Christ; in every circumstance we can approach the throne of grace boldly. Jesus wants to be your solution; include Him in every situation, good or bad.

4. *Keep our eyes open for "divine detours"*

- Jesus had a plan to heal Jairus' daughter, but took an opportunity to restore a woman in need. Like Jesus, we need to keep our eyes open for ministry opportunities.

The Bible describes faith as being *sure* of what we do not see. Faith doesn't make us falsely optimistic, but faith renews our minds. Our renewed mind allows us to focus on Jesus and not the storm. Faith allows us to trust in God's promises, when we do not see the plan or final result. We reign in faith because turning to Jesus empowers us. We reign in faith because we know that with God all things are possible. Faith is simply trusting God to gain victory on your behalf.

Spiritual Discipline in Action

As we trust God to gain victory on our behalf, remember God can use "just a little" faith to move mountains. "Little faith" reminds me of a sweet story my friend shared after substitute teaching a first grade class. The kids where returning to class from lunch and a student runs to her and asked: "Are you a Christian Ms. Tena?" She replies with a "yes" and the students says, "I am too." Full of excitement, the student goes on to ask her what's her spirical birthday? She gently responds with "what do you mean?" He replies, "The day you became a Christian?" Realizing he meant spiritual birthday, she shared she didn't know the exact day, but was 9 years old when she became a Christian.

He responded, "I have a spirical birthday! It was Thanksgiving!" It was September, so Ms. Tena asked if he had become a Christian last Thanksgiving. He said "No, this year! It was during lunch recess!" So Ms. Tena is excited but confused and asked, "Wait, where and who told you?" Then he had the most precious response: "My best friend prayed with me in the sandbox. He's my neighbor too!" He's a first grader. But, the story doesn't end here; he goes on to share his faith with another student. Ms. Tena couldn't hear the entire conversation, but she hears him saying Jesus' name, folding their hands, and pointing to the heart. She overheard him say, as they repeated, the words; "Jesus," "door", and "in my heart." Wow, out of the mouth of babes!

Are you crying yet? This young boy shared his faith with two friends that day. And he had just (literally) celebrated his "spirical birthday!" Learn a lesson from these first graders. If a first grader can lead his friend to Christ in the sandbox, we can surely share our faith with others. The *spiritual discipline of witness* moves us to be intentional in telling others about Christ.

Discipline—*Witness*

Purpose: To reveal through modeling and/or telling others what God has done in your life.

Go, therefore, and make disciples of all nations, baptizing them in the name of the Father and of the Son and of the Holy Spirit, teaching them to observe everything I have commanded you. And remember, I am with you always, to the end of the age (Matthew 28:19-20 HCSB).

The Great Commission

Jesus commands us all to go out into the world and make disciples. Like any command of God, we are also empowered to evangelize and share our testimony to the world. We can start with our family, friends, classmates, and co-workers. You have a story to tell, and the world needs to hear it.

Start With Writing Your Story—Take 10 min. and pray for God to reveal your testimony. Ask Him to reveal the ways of your life before fully committing to Him. Ask God to reveal the process in which you came to believe. And finally ask God to reveal the changes that have occurred in your life after becoming a true disciple. Your story is not complete; however, many will be impacted and encouraged by what God is currently doing in your life.

Write it Down—After praying, write out what God has brought to your heart. Spend 20 min. in developing your honest testimony to share with others.

I.   **Before Committing to Christ**
   a.   What did your life look like?
   b.   What did you focus on the most?
   c.   Did you feel a need for God?
   d.   If you grew up in a Christian Home, start from there. "I grew up in a Christian home..."

II.   **The Process**
   a.   Who shared Christ with you?
   b.   When was it clear that Jesus is real?
   c.   How did it feel to accept and believe in Christ completely?
   d.   Did you experience a dynamic encounter with Jesus?

III. After Committing to Christ
    a. What difference do you see in your life after believing in Christ?
    b. How has God renewed your thoughts and thinking?
    c. Why should others also believe in Jesus?

Finally Pray—Pray for God to give you the courage to share your testimony. Ask God to open doors for you to share His goodness with your loved ones. Keep your eyes open for "divine detours" where God's delay may be an opening to witness to someone.

Chapter Overview

1. Repentance involves negative and positive principles: the negative—turning from sin and the positive—turning to God.

2. Faith is belief, trust, or confidence in a person or idea. We all display some level of faith every day.

3. Bibles gives examples of false faith, head faith, see it faith, and dead faith.

4. God desires for us to have soul saving faith. God desires a faith that not only turns to Jesus for salvation, but also walks with Him for the rest of our lives.

5. Jesus explains that with just a "little faith" we can do the impossible.

6. Jesus taught the principle of faith in various parables, especially the parable of the sower. God desires that our hearts be fertile and good soil.

7. Faith is turning to Jesus, but also fixing our eyes on Him.

Related Scriptures

- Psalm 31:23
- 2 Peter 1:5-7
- Romans 14:23
- Hebrews 12:2
- 1 Timothy 6:12

CHAPTER 9

Reign in Your Purpose

The Lord will fulfill his purpose for me; your steadfast love,
O Lord, endures forever
(Psalm 138:8 ESV).

We were created with the purpose to relate, reflect, and reign. When we witness and share the works of God in our lives, we operate in all three R's. We relate with others by sharing the goodness of God. We reflect God as we model His character. Finally, we reign by walking with God and living the life He created us to live. Your testimony matters and the world needs to hear it. You were placed within your family, your school, your workplace, and your church for *such a time as this*. No one else can do what you were created to do. This is the time to live in your full potential and purpose. This is the time to allow your life to reflect your creator and a time to make the most of your life.

For Such a Time as This

Queen Esther is a great example of a woman who made the most of her time. Esther was a young Jewish girl who lived with her older cousin Mordecai in Susa, Persia. Mordecai was like a father to Esther since the death of her parents. King Ahasuerus ruled the land and was in search for a new queen. He held somewhat of a beauty pageant to find his new queen. All the young women in town signed up for a chance to win the throne. Esther was beautiful and pondered the chance to be queen. However, there was one issue, Esther was Jewish. At that time, Jews were forbidden to marry non-Jews. The possibility of being a part of the King's harem also violated rules of sexual purity before marriage. Yet, Mordecai allowed Ester to enter into the contest and she won! Esther found favor and approval from the King. The King loved Esther and made her his queen.

Each day Mordecai sat at the King's Gate. The gate was like a trade center, where legal and commercial deals were made. One day Mordecai refused to bow down and pay homage to a man named Haman, King Ahasuerus' highest-ranking official. The King commanded all to pay respect to Haman, but Mordecai would not bow down to him. Mordecai continued to disobey the King's order day after day. Haman soon became infuriated and made plans to punish Mordecai. However, Haman learned Mordecai was a Jew, and he was not content with punishing Mordecai alone. Haman planned to annihilate all Jews throughout the kingdom.

Then Haman said to King Xerxes, "There is a certain people dispersed among the peoples in all the provinces of your kingdom who keep themselves separate. Their customs are different from those of all other people, and they do not obey the king's laws; it is not in the king's best interest to tolerate them. If it pleases the king, let a decree be issued to destroy them, and I will give ten thousand talents of silver to the king's administrators for the royal treasury" (Esther 3:8-9).

Haman offered to pay an equivalent of millions of dollars to destroy the Jews. The King saw Haman's offers as devotion to him. He agreed and signed a decree to destroy the Jews. The King also told Haman to keep the money and do as he pleased with the Jews. Meanwhile, the decree was sent throughout the province and sent the kingdom into frenzy. Mordecai and all the Jews of the land were distressed and cried out to the Lord.

Esther's female servants came and reported the news to her. She became overwhelmed with fear and sent for Mordecai. Mordecai refused, but told Esther's servant all that had gone on. Mordecai gave the servant a copy of the King's decree and instructed Esther to go before the King to plea for her people. However, Esther had never revealed her nationality to the King or anyone in the palace.

Ester's Response

All the king's officials and the people of the royal provinces know that for any man or woman who approaches the king in the inner court without being summoned the king has but one law: that they be put to death unless the king extends the gold scepter to them and spares their lives. But thirty days have passed since I was called to go to the king (Esther 4:11)

Mordecai's Response

Do not think that because you are in the king's house you alone of all the Jews will escape. For if you remain silent at this time, relief and deliverance for the Jews will arise from another place, but you and your father's family will perish. And who knows but that you have come to your royal position for such a time as this? (Ester 4:13-14).

Esther sent a messenger to Mordecai and told him to gather all the people to fast and pray for her. Esther needed courage and the hand of God to intervene. She knew going before the King unsolicited could result in death. Three days later, Esther went before the King. She dressed in fine royal linens, hoping her beauty would win over the King. As she approached the King's courtyard, she trembled and each step became more difficult. The King just happened to be on his throne in the courtroom facing the courtyard. As Esther entered the courtyard the King saw her and was in awe. Instantly Esther won his approval!

She found favor with the King and eventually was able to save her people. Haman was punished for his actions and Mordecai was given his estate. Esther's story outlines courage, but also teaches the importance of your current life position. *For such a time as this*, you are exactly where God needs you.

If not you . . . then who? Who will step in and complete your purpose? Mordecai shared with Esther, *"deliverance for the Jews will arise from another place, but you and your father's family will perish."* There are consequences for disobedience. Fear to step into your purpose will not only negatively affect you, but others also. For Esther, the livelihood of an entire nation was at stake. What's at stake in your life? It may feel difficult or nearly impossible to live in your purpose because of the current season you are in. Relationships, jobs, and finances may hold you back from living in your true purpose. However, when we step into our purpose, God is also there.

You Are an Ambassador

So we are Christ's ambassadors; God is making his appeal through us. We speak for Christ when we plead, "Come back to God!" (2 Corinthians 5:20 NLT).

Like Esther, we were created to stand for what is right and true. The Bible calls us "Ambassadors," through whom God speaks to save others. An ambassador is the highest-ranking diplomat sent as an official representative to a foreign country. In the natural an ambassador's purpose is to represent a country as a resident in a foreign land. As an ambassador for Christ, our role is to represent Him. You are a high-ranking diplomat sent from God to earth. You were sent to your family, school, career, and church to represent God. *For such a time as this* and right where you are, you have a purpose.

Reflection Questions

1. *We are citizens of heaven, where the Lord Jesus Christ lives. And we are eagerly waiting for him to return as our Savior* (Philippians 3:20 NLT). Paul reminds us that we are citizens of Heaven, and we are Ambassadors for Christ. What does the title of Ambassador reveal about your purpose?

2. Where has God currently placed you to represent Him as an Ambassador? And, what do you believe God has called you to specifically do in these places?

3. As a foreign officer, an Ambassador is also expected to serve through promoting peace and protecting the citizens of his home country. How has God called you to protect others or promote peace in your current circumstance?

Your Testimony Matters

You are an Ambassador everywhere you go. You are an Ambassador to your family, to your friends, and to those you interact with every day. God has called you to relate, reflect, and reign as an Ambassador. God has commissioned and equipped you to serve as His highest-ranking diplomat. He has sent you to represent Him to an on looking world. This is a big deal! No pressure but God has great expectations for you. He knows you can do it, and He has equipped you with the ability to fulfill your purpose. So what does being an Ambassador look like in your life? How should you step into this position? Where should you start?

Right where you are! God will use you as ambassador for Him right where you are and in your current circumstance. We can learn this lesson from an unnamed character in the book of John called the Samaritan Woman. The woman's title "Samaritan" is important because the Samaritan people were a mixed race people. The Samaritans were of both Jewish and Assyrian heritage. The Samaritans adopted many of the Jewish religious costumes, however many Jews continued to look down upon them. Many viewed the land of Samaria as unclean, and tried to avoid the area all together. However, Jesus had a special mission in the land of Samaria.

Jesus and the Samaritan Woman

Jesus traveled through Samaria on His way to Galilee. While in the land of Samaria, Jesus stopped and rested at a well. While Jesus rested, a Samaritan woman came to the well and drew water. Jesus asked the woman for a drink, and the woman responded in shock. The woman was shocked because Jesus, a Jewish man, spoke to her. *"How is it that You, a Jew, ask for a drink from me, a Samaritan woman?" she asked Him. For Jews do not associate with Samaritans"* (John 4:9 HCSB).

REIGN IN YOUR PURPOSE • 123

Jesus' Response

> *Jesus answered, "If you knew the gift of God, and who*
> *is saying to you, 'Give Me a drink,' you would ask Him,*
> *and He would give you living water (John 4:10 HCSB).*

      Jesus had broken Jewish tradition by traveling through Samaria. Jesus continued to break ethnic and religious customs by associating with a Samaritan. Then Jesus sets the stage to offer the Samaritans living water. Jesus is vague in His offering, but still draws the woman in. She is interested, but still not sure what this "living water" truly is. Jesus explains how the water He offers leads to eternal life. Immediately, the woman is intrigued and wants this water. She thinks who is this guy? Is He a prophet? Or is He just flat out crazy? Jesus' next statement makes it clear who He really is.

> *"Go call your husband," He told her, "and come back*
> *here." "I don't have a husband," she answered. "You*
> *have correctly said, 'I don't have a husband,'" Jesus*
> *said. "For you've had five husbands, and the man you*
> *now have is not your husband. What you have said is*
> *true" (John 4: 17-28 HCSB).*

      At that moment, the woman knew Jesus was a prophet. She knew only the one sent from God would know the truth about her life. They continued a dialogue about faith and worship, and then the woman mentioned the coming Messiah. She lit up with hope when she mentioned Him. She knew relations between the Samaritans and the Jews would be restored at His arrival. She knew He would clarify the true meaning of worship. She exclaims, *"When He comes, He will explain everything to us."* Then Jesus reveals *"I am He,"* . . . *"the One speaking to you."*

The Samaritans Woman's Response

Then the woman left her water jar, went into town, and told the men, "Come, see a man who told me everything I ever did! Could this be the Messiah?" They left the town and made their way to Him (John 4: 28-30 HCSB).

The Result

Now many Samaritans from that town believed in Him because of what the woman said when she testified, "He told me everything I ever did." Therefore, when the Samaritans came to Him, they asked Him to stay with them, and He stayed there two days. Many more believed because of what He said. And they told the woman, "We no longer believe because of what you said, for we have heard for ourselves and know that this really is the Savior of the world (John 4:39-42 HCSB).

Because of What the Woman Said

Because of what the woman said, many of her people came to believe in Jesus. They too received the living water He offers. Because of what she said, they can live in the promise of eternal life. Their sins will be forgiven, and they too can live in their divine purpose as an Ambassador. All because this woman shared what Jesus did for her. She wasn't perfect and didn't have all of the answers. She simply couldn't keep this great news to herself.

God Uses the Imperfect

Even in sin, God used the Samaritan Woman to save her people. Jesus revealed her dark past of failed relationships. She had 5 failed marriages, and currently living with a man she wasn't married to. Could you imagine the heartbreak she experienced? Could you imagine feelings of not being good enough, feelings of despair, and loneliness? This woman was broken and thirsty for something to fill a void. She filled the void of loneliness and despair with men. After the fifth try, she said forget it! Why get married? So she settled, as many women often do, and continued to live outside of her purpose.

But God met her right where she was. God met her in her mess! She met the man that could provide a never-ending supply of living water. She met the man that brought purpose and direction to her life. And she met the man who could save her people. God used this woman not only to save the Samaritans, but also to break the social stigma of associating with them. Jesus showed His disciples and the entire world that we are all equal. We are all equally in need of a Savior. Jesus tore down racial barriers that separated the Jews from Gentiles. Jesus stayed with the Samaritans and restored them as fully human, to a world who viewed them as less than. All because of what she said!

What Do You Have to Say?

Who would believe a woman with five failed marriages? Or believe a woman with a promiscuous past? The Samaritan woman could have allowed her current circumstance to keep her from sharing her story. She could have allowed thoughts of inadequacy or shame keep her silent. Yet, she dropped her belongings and ran to tell all who would listen. What has God done for you that the world needs to hear about? What has God delivered you from? What void has God filled, that was once occupied by sin?

God can and will use those areas to help save others. Like the Samaritan woman, God will use you in spite of your past. She was broken and living in sin, however, the living water allowed her to be forgiven and set free to tell others about the Messiah. God will also use your past as an instrument to relate and save others from similar circumstances.

Failed relationships, miscarriages, drug abuse, lying, abortion, promiscuity, a harsh tongue, sexual abuse, depression, etc., God can use to win others to Christ. Your unique testimony is an essential piece to your purpose. No one can impact others the way you will. Let your voice be heard as an Ambassador for Christ!

Reflection Questions

1. What unique experiences have you encountered? How can these experiences be used to encourage others?

2. What areas of service do you feel most passionate about? (Children, women, families, elderly, disabled persons, etc.) How do you see God calling you to serve in those areas?

3. If you were to dream and created a job description including both your unique experiences and passion to serve, what would it look like? (Create a name for the position, and then write your duties and responsibilities.

I. Job Title_____

II. Job Description

    A. Purpose

        _____

        _____

        _____

    B. Duties & Responsibilities

        _____

        _____

        _____

        _____

        _____

Spiritual Discipline in Action

When I returned from my mission trip to Ghana, I was overwhelmed by the provision of God. He not only provided for the trip, but He also awakened the ministry He placed inside me. One morning after the amazing high of the trip, I sat at my desk and admitted to myself: "I need to do missions every day!" I didn't believe God was calling me to a long-term mission trip, but He was calling me into fulltime ministry. I had no clue what it would look like, but the desire to serve the Lord full time was undeniable.

I began to pray and ask God to help me see a vision for myself, and how I would fit in to fulltime ministry. "I'm a girl and single, who will hire me?" These questions gave me doubt that I could actually make a living in ministry. I thought maybe I would have to work a secular job and do ministry on the side. In fact, this is what I was already doing. I worked 9-5, and finally got to what I really wanted to do: tell people about Jesus.

Realizing this pattern left me unfulfilled and searching to do more with my time; I prayed for God to open doors for me in ministry. God eventually called me to make one of the hardest decisions of my life. Quit my job, not having a job to go to. Yikes! My dad advised me not to leave my job until I'd secured another. Even my boss wanted me to have something to move on to before quitting. However, my heavenly Father was calling me to trust Him again. After all, He had just proven Himself as a provider with my mission's trip; why not trust Him now?

So I resigned and I humbly moved back home with my parents. A month later, I called Fellowship of Christian Athletes, an international sports ministry, to inquire about volunteering at my old high school. This call rocked my world! I called in hopes of volunteering; however, the Director for the local FCA stated: "We have been praying for a female staffer, let's meet and talk about potentially joining the staff." Seven years later, I continue to serve in full time ministry with FCA!

The spiritual discipline of *sharing your desires with God* opens our communication through intentional efforts to share our most intimate thoughts with God. Let's take some time to share our desires with God.

Discipline—*Sharing your desires with God*
Purpose: To share your heart's desires and passions with God. Sharing your desires with God is an intentional effort to disclose your most intimate thoughts with God; even if you are not sure your desires are in line with His will and purpose

for your life. Sharing your desires allows two-way communication between God and you. You share your heart, and He will give you direction.

> **Take 10 min.** to look over your "Dream Job" description and pray for God to reveal ways to incorporate your unique experiences and passions into serving others.

> **Take 20 min.** to pray and share with God the desires of your heart. Share your hopes and dreams with Him. Disclose your desires for your relationships, career, family, education, and even areas of healing and restoration. Finally pray for God to reveal your true passions and how to use those passions to serve others.

Chapter Overview

1. When we witness and share the works of God in our lives, we operate in all three R's (Relate, Reflect, and Reign).

2. Your testimony matters and the world needs to hear it. You were placed within your family, your school, your workplace, and your church for *such a time as this*.

3. You are exactly where you need to be. God will use you to serve your friends and family.

4. Relationships, jobs, and finances may hold you back from living in your true purpose. However, when we step into our purpose, God is also there.

5. Queen Esther made the most of her position as queen by standing for what's right and saving her people.

6. The Bible calls us *Ambassadors*, through whom God speaks to save others. An ambassador is a highest-ranking diplomat sent as an official repre-sentative to a foreign country. As an ambassador for Christ, our role is to represent Him.

7. The Samaritan woman saved many from her land and also broke down racial barriers between the Jews and Samaritans by witnessing to others about Jesus.

8. God can use your past to help save others in similar circumstances.

Related Scriptures

- Jeremiah 29:11
- Matthew 6:33
- Matthew 28:19-20
- Romans 8:28
- Romans 12:2
- Colossians 3:23

CHAPTER 10

Reign in the Body of Christ

*All of you together are Christ's body,
and each of you is a part of it*
(1 Corinthians 12:27 NLT).

God has placed you right where you are for such a time as this. This is not by chance, but by God's grace. Even your mistakes will be used to glorify God and bring salvation to others. The amazing thing about God's grace is that when we repent, we not only turn to Him, but to our purpose. God's sovereign hand has always been in control. *We know that all things work together for the good of those who love God: those who are called according to His purpose* (Romans 8:28 HCSB). God knew how Paul's unique experience as a Pharisee and persecutor of Christians would help him teach about God's forgiveness. God knew how the woman who bled for 12 twelve years would teach others to make God their first option. And God knew the Samaritan woman would spread the gospel to her people and begin to break barriers of racial inequalities. Their testimonies are still relevant today. However, God also knows the impact of your unique ministry.

I knew you before I formed you in your mother's womb. Before you were born I set you apart (Jeremiah 1:5 NLT).

God knows how awesome you are. He knows your personality, talents, passions, and desires. He knows what fulfills you and knows the burdens of your heart. He knew these things before He formed you. He knew what your unique ministry would be before your parents knew of your existence. He formed you with your specific passions and talents in mind. God also created your personal design with the Body of Christ in mind.

The Body of Christ

The body of Christ is an analogy Paul used to describe all true believers of Christ. Paul compared the many parts of the human body to individual believers in Christ. Paul explains how all the parts are different and each serve a unique purpose to the proper functioning and health of the body. *Just as our bodies have many parts and each part has a special function, so it is with Christ's body. We are many parts of one body, and we all belong to each other* (Romans 12:4-5 NLT). You have a special part and function within the body of Christ. Discovering your role within the body of Christ reveals your specific ministry.

A Called Minister?

Many view the role of *Minister* as a special group of people who are called to serve the church. This special group of people is set apart for theological study and teaching. They represent God and encourage others to believe and follow Him. Wait, this sounds a bit like you. Have you not been called by God with a specific purpose to serve others? Are you not an ambassador for Christ, sent to represent God? Yes! The word *ministry* may be a bit intimidating but you are indeed a minister.

    Ministry is simply a service you have been set apart to do. Every member of the body of Christ has a ministry or service that is vital to the body. Here Paul expounds on the diversity of service amongst the body.

> *If the foot says, "I am not a part of the body because I am not a hand," that does not make it any less a part of the body. And if the ear says, "I am not part of the body because I am not an eye," would that make it any less a part of the body? If the whole body were an eye, how would you hear? Or if your whole body were an ear, how would you smell anything?*
>
> *But our bodies have many parts, and God has put each part just where he wants it. How strange a body would be if it had only one part! Yes, there are many parts, but only one body (1 Corinthians 12:15-20 NLT).*

Like the hand, ear, and eye have a different but important function; all members of Christ's body have a different but important role. In order for the body to function at its best, all the parts must do its part. In order for the body of Christ to be as strong and effective, we must do our part. Identifying your role allows you to be effective in the right place. Could you imagine an ear trying to be a hand? No, that would be silly! Yet often within the body of Christ, we attempt to be something we're not. We attempt to fill roles we weren't created for. God has a specific purpose for you that only you can do. Only your gifts and passions can fulfill this role effectively. So how do we identify our role in the body? And how do we operate within the function we were created for? We do so by identifying our spiritual gifts.

Spiritual Gifts

Spiritual gifts are abilities given by the Spirit of God to accomplish our spiritual service to the body of Christ. Spiritual gifts differ from natural ability or talents. Talents are abilities or capabilities one receives naturally and at birth. For example one may possess the natural ability to sing well or soar in athletics. On the other hand, spiritual gifts are given to born again believers in Christ. Spiritual gifts are an expression of the Holy Spirit that dwells inside us and empowers us to minister effectively. Whatever God calls us to do; He will empower us to do so. Our spiritual gifts are the channel through which we execute our role in God's redemption plan for the world. God can and will utilize your natural gifts to glorify Him and help win others over for Christ. Often times your natural gifts are complementary to your spiritual gifts; however, your spiritual gifts are specific to Christian service.

In his grace, God has given us different gifts for doing certain things well. So if God has given you the ability to prophesy, speak out with as much faith as God has given you. If your gift is serving others, serve them well. If you are a teacher, teach well. If your gift is to encourage others, be encouraging. If it is giving, give generously. If God has given you leadership ability, take the responsibility seriously. And if you have a gift for showing kindness to others, do it gladly (Romans 12:6-8 NLT).

The Holy Spirit graciously gives spiritual gifts to every believer. Every believer has a spiritual gift that is vital to the Body of Christ. Yet, many believers are unaware of their gifts. So it is our job to discover the unique spiritual gifts God has given to us in order to exercise them. The Bible highlights and defines the various spiritual gifts. Let's take a look at these roles and gifts given to the body of Christ.

Leadership (Romans 12:8)—The spiritual gift of leadership aids the church by providing clear vision and direction in order to meet specific goals. Those with the gift of leadership use their gifts to communicate clear goals. These leaders often tend to be the "point person" because of their ability to motivate others to take action.

Administration (1 Corinthians 12:28)—Those with the spiritual gift of administration lead by organizing and keeping members on task. The gift of administration has the unique ability to help leaders of the body of Christ determine goals and then create an action plan to accomplish goals orderly.

Teaching (Romans 12:7, Ephesians 4:11, & 1 Corinthians 12:28)—The gift of teaching enables one to understand and teach biblical truth. Many may possess the natural gift of teaching, but the spiritual gift of teaching focuses on teaching the Bible. Those with the gift of teaching are also able to make biblical truth relevant and provide personal application.

Pastor (Ephesians 4:11)—The spiritual gift of Pastoring drives one to care for the spiritual welfare of others. The word *pastor* means shepherd, which involves caring and nurturing the body of Christ like a shepherd would his flock. Pastors help to nurture and mature the spiritual lives of their members. The position of pastor is often associated with professional ministry, such as a head pastor or church staff; but is not limited to vocational ministry. Women as well as other laypeople (non-church staff) possess the gift of shepherding. These people have a passion for the health of the church and desire to protect the flock of Christ.

Prophecy (1 Corinthians 12:10 & Romans 12:6)—The spiritual gift of prophecy is the desire and ability to proclaim the truth of God boldly. The ability to speak God's truth, even on tough topics, builds up the body and convicts hearts to repent from sin. Prophecy is most commonly manifested through teaching and preaching the Bible.

Apostleship (1 Corinthians 12:28 & Ephesians 4:11)—Those with the gift of apostleship have the ability and vision to launch ministries outside of the local church. Often those with the gift of apostleship are sent from their local churches to plant new churches or be missionaries. Those with the gift of apostleship have a desire for the world to know and hear the gospel of Christ.

Evangelism (Ephesians 4:11)—Evangelism is the spiritual ability to clearly communicate the gospel of Christ, resulting in unbelievers accepting Christ. Those with the gift of evangelism have a passion for speaking about Christ and a desire that the entire world be saved. Their passion for people, who do not know Christ, makes them effective in connecting and building trust with unbelievers. They strengthen the body of Christ by adding new members.

Encouragement (Romans 12:8)—Those with the gift of encouragement are "motivators." They have the unique ability to encourage members of the body to draw closer to Christ and take action in service. They are able to encourage the discouraged and many are drawn to seek counsel from them. Encouragers also have the great ability of confronting tough issues with love. They are able to admonish members without tearing them down, restoring the member into the body.

Discernment (1 Corinthians 12:10)—The spiritual gift of discernments aids the body by identifying truth from falsehood. Those with discernment have the unique ability to recognize the true intention of others amongst the body. Those with the gift of discernment are able to distinguish what drives others, God, self, or Satan. This protects the wellbeing of the body by testing the words and actions of others.

Faith (1 Corinthians 12:9)—Those with the spiritual gift of faith demonstrate supernatural ability to trust God. They have strong confidence in the power and provision of God, even in difficult times. Those with this level of faith also have the ability to encourage others to trust in God.

Service/ Helps (Romans 12:7 and 1 Corinthians 12:28)—Those with the spiritual gift of service have the ability to recognize a need in the body, and then joyfully provide help to accomplish the task. Those with the gift of service or helps do not mind working behind the scenes or not receiving recognition for their work. Those with the gift of service make things "happen" within the body by freeing up others by stepping in to help.

Hospitality (1 Peter 4:9)—Those with the gift of hospitality strengthen the body by integrating new members and making them feel like family. They have a divine gift to make others feel comfortable and welcomed. They enjoy entertaining others in their home and the church.

Mercy (Romans 12:8)—Those with the spiritual gift of mercy possess the unique ability to feel and empathize with others. Mercy pushes them to feel the pain of others, and compassion moves them to do all they can to help. Those with the gift of mercy help to build the body by bringing awareness to the needs within the body.

Giving (Romans 12:8)—Members with the spiritual gift of giving give cheerfully of their time and financial resources. The generosity builds the body by giving selflessly of their resources. They find joy in meeting the needs of others. These givers also strengthen the body by providing the resources needed to accomplish goals.

Reign in Your Domain

Spiritual gifts are divine gifts from God, a heavenly gift that enables us to be successful in Christian service. God hand selected these gifts for you and knew just what you needed to accomplish your unique purpose. Discovering your spiritual gifts allows you to reign in the domain God created you for. Knowing how God has gifted you allows you to be effective in the right place. Finally, serving in your domain will bring authentic joy and fulfillment in your life. So know what's next? How do we identify the unique spiritual gifts we possess? How do we begin to put them in action? Prayer, Study, and Survey.

Spiritual Discipline in Action

Discipline—*Pray, Study, Survey*
Purpose: Spending intentional time and focus on discovering your spiritual gifts.

Prayer -*This is why I remind you to fan into flames the spiritual gift God gave you* (2 Timothy 1:6 NLT).

Paul encouraged Timothy, a young pastor, to fan the flame of his spiritual gifts. Paul encouraged Timothy to make the most of what God had given to him. Likewise, we must trust that God has indeed given us a divine gift, then we must fan that flame to ignite into a forest fire, a forest fire that casts light unto a dark and lost world. And a fire that warms and fills your heart for serving in your purpose.

So now we must spend time in intentional prayer for God to reveal our spiritual gifts. Ask God to help you identify the gifts you are attracted to and the gifts that fit your passions and personality. Finally, pray for God to help you understand the various gifts and reveal ways to take action.

Study—*Your word is a lamp to my feet and a light to my path* (Psalm 119:105 ESV).

Spiritual gifts are an expression of the Holy Spirit that dwells within you. The Word of God will illuminate how this expression should be put to use through you. In addition to prayer, in order to discover your divine gifting, you also must prayerfully explore the scripture. Study and pray for understanding of the passages that list and explain the various gifts. You can start by taking time to look over the definitions listed in this chapter, as well as study the related scriptures.

Survey—*Each of you should use whatever gift you have received to serve others, as faithful stewards of God's grace in its various forms* (1 Peter 4:10).

Finally we must examine ourselves to assess the gifts that are already present in our lives. We are able to assess our personal gifting through *Spiritual Gifts Inventory Tests*. The tests provide a personalized analysis through questionnaire style testing. The great thing about this test is there are no right or wrong answers. This discovery tool allows you to take a step closer to identifying your gifts. Your *Spiritual Discipline in Action* for the week is to complete the *Spiritual Gifts Inventory* in Appendix A.

Chapter Overview

1. God also knows the impact of your unique ministry. He has also equipped you to fulfill your purpose effectively.

2. God created you with the Body of Christ in mind. The Body of Christ is a metaphor that represents all true believers of Christ.

3.   The human body is made up of many parts with unique functions, similarly the body of Christ is made up of many parts, and you have a unique role to play.

4.   Ministry means service, and you have a specific ministry to serve the body of Christ. God has equipped you with spiritual gifts to serve the body.

5.   Spiritual gifts are abilities given by the Spirit of God to accomplish our spiritual service to the body of Christ.

6.   Ephesians, 1 Corinthians, Romans, and 1 Peter are replete with lists and examples of the various spiritual gifts.

7.   We must take time and focus in prayer and study of the Word of God to reveal our unique spiritual gifts. Inventory tests will also help in identifying your gifts.

Related Scriptures

- Romans 12:6-8
- 1 Corinthians 12:8-10
- Ephesians 4:11
- 1 Peter 4:9-11

CHAPTER 11

Reign Through Serving

*You, my brothers and sisters, were called to be free. But do
not use your freedom to indulge the flesh; rather,
serve one another humbly in love*
(Galatians 5:13).

Isn't it awesome how God involves us in His work? How
He shares His image and ministry with us?   He doesn't
need us, but wants us to share in His glory. God wants
you! He wants a relationship with you. He wants you to
reflect Him fully. He wants you to reign! Everything God has
done, from creation to redemption, is because He wants you!
He wants you to be the person He created you to be. He wants
you to have the abundant life He created for you to live. So,
how does it feel to be wanted by God? How does it feel to be
chosen?

You are so special to God and vital to the body of
Christ. No one else can do what you were called to do. As a
woman you bring a unique and powerful perspective to the
body of Christ. Some may overlook the impact of women in
ministry, however you are needed. Throughout the Bible,
women have contributed to the work of God. The book of
Luke highlights the contributions of women to Jesus' the
earthly ministry (Luke 8).   In the book of Romans, Paul
praises the women who served alongside him in ministry:

I commend to you our sister Phoebe, who is a deacon in the church in Cenchrea. Welcome her in the Lord as one who is worthy of honor among God's people. Help her in whatever she needs, for she has been helpful to many, and especially to me.

Give my greetings to Priscilla and Aquila, my co-workers in the ministry of Christ Jesus. In fact, they once risked their lives for me. I am thankful to them, and so are all the Gentile churches. Also give my greetings to the church that meets in their home.

Greet my dear friend Epenetus. He was the first person from the province of Asia to become a follower of Christ. Give my greetings to Mary, who has worked so hard for your benefit.

Greet Andronicus and Junia, my fellow Jews, who were in prison with me. They are highly respected among the apostles and became followers of Christ before I did . . .

Give my greetings to Tryphena and Tryphosa, the Lord's workers, and to dear Persis, who has worked so hard for the Lord. Greet Rufus, whom the Lord picked out to be his very own; and also his dear mother, who has been a mother to me.

Give my greetings to Philologus, Julia, Nereus and his sister, and to Olympas and all the believers who meet with them (Romans 16:1-7, 12-13, 15 NLT).

Romans 16

Chapter 16 is the final chapter of the book of Romans. Often times the concluding chapter of an epistle or letter gave the final greeting. Many overlook the greetings because it consists of difficult names and lacks theological meat. However, Romans 16 means so much to a woman discovering their ministry and place in the body of Christ.

In My Pastor's Office

One day my Pastor called me into his office to check-in and follow up on a few projects. Before getting into the details of work, he wanted to spend time in a devotional reading. He began to read Romans Chapter 16, and I began to weep. I mean big baby, snotty nose weep. As he hands me tissue, he asked "What's going on?" I had so much going on at the time. It was my first year of seminary, and my place in ministry was constantly being challenged. From my peers, to textbooks, I was made to feel women had no place in full time ministry. I worried if I was doing something wrong.

After I gathered composure, we continued reading. He explained how out of a list of 27 names in chapter 16, 10 were women. Paul not only listed their names, but also praised them for their ministry. He affirmed them and urged others to honor and respect their service to the body of Christ. Paul also gave hints to their spiritual gifts.

Women Serving in Their Spiritual Gifts

- **Phoebe** (16:1, 2)—Phoebe was a deaconess in the church of Cenchrea. The word *deaconess* or *diakonos* in the New Testament Greek means servant, minister, or administrator. Phoebe served alongside Paul and is also believe to have delivered this very letter to the church at Rome. Paul commissioned others to honor her and help her in whatever she needed. **Spiritual Gifts**—Administration and Service.

- **Pricilla** (16:3-5)—Pricilla and her husband Aquila were greeted as "co-workers" in ministry. Pricilla's name being mentioned before her husband's notes that she played a more visible role in their ministry. Pricilla and Aquila trained Apollos, one the New Testament's prominent teachers. They also led a church in their home. **Spiritual Gifts**—Teacher, Pastor, Apostleship, and Hospitality.

- **Mary** (16:6)—Mary was the sister of Martha and Lazarus. Mary and her family had a great relationship with Jesus. Mary continued in ministry after the resurrection of Christ. Paul noted that she worked hard or *kopiaó* in Greek, which means *diligently labor*. **Spiritual gifts**—Service.

- **Junia** (16:7)—Junia and her husband Andronicus were apostles who had seen the risen Christ. Junia and Andronicus were missionaries Paul praised for their outstanding work in ministry.
  Spiritual Gifts—Apostleship and Evangelism.

- **Trypheana, Tryphosa and Persis** (16:12)—Trypheana and Tryphosa were sisters who served together in ministry. Persis or "Persian Woman" served the ministry and was beloved by the Roman Christians. Paul praised all three women for their hard work in the ministry. **Spiritual Gifts**—Service.

- **Rufus' Mother** (16:13)—Paul praised Rufus' mother for being a mother figure to him. Even a man like Paul benefited from the welcoming presence of an older mother figure. **Spiritual Gifts**—Hospitality.

- **Julia and Nereus' Sister** (16:15)—Julia and Nereus' sister are greeted as saints and members of the body of Christ. **Spiritual Gifts:** Faith.

The Call

Paul gave a glimpse of his view of women and ministry in Chapter 16 of Romans. These women were beneficial to Paul's ministry and vital to the body of Christ. They helped bring the gospel of Christ to their friends and family. They traveled to teach about Jesus and planted new churches. They started churches in their homes. They served Paul and other church leaders through giving and hospitality. They were co-workers in ministry with Paul. Even when Paul could not remember their names, Paul still acknowledged their work and wanted to bring honor to their service. These women responded to the call placed upon their life. I am proud to follow in their footsteps and also respond to the call God has placed on my life. You too have a call on your life. This call of God is to live out your purpose as mighty women to serve a mighty God.

The call on your life can be divided into three categories—*General* Call, *Individual* Call and, the *Right Now* Call. The *General* call is call for all of God's creation. The general call is to relate with God and have an intimate relationship with Him. To relate with others in a way that brings God glory. Reflecting the image of God is also a mission of our call to love and honor God. Next our *Individual Call* is how we uniquely relate to others and reflect God. We reign when we identify our individual call, and begin to live in our passions, talents, and spiritual gifts. Finally, the *right now call* is your calling in your current life circumstance. God may call you to relate and reflect Him in other ways according to the stages of your life. Your "*right now*" calling is similar to Esther's *for such a time as this*. Singleness, marriage, and motherhood may all require something new of us. These stages of life are all a part of God's unique plan for you

A Life of Service

The "Proverbs 31 Woman" is a great example of a *life of service*. Many look at the example of this virtuous woman and become overwhelmed at the thought of her capability and accomplishments to the point of deeming her unattainable and not a real woman. It's deemed unrealistic for her to accomplish all she did while being a wife and mother. She was a successful wife and mother while being an:

- Entrepreneur—v. 18, 23
- Financial investor—v. 18
- Realtor and Landlord—v. 16
- Designer and seamstress of her own clothing and bed linen—v. 22
- Influential teacher—v. 26
- World Traveler—v. 14
- Merchant to tradesmen—v. 24
- Avid Gardener—v. 16
- Philanthropist—v. 20

She accomplished all this while staying up late and waking up before sunrise. Her husband and children praised her and thought the world of her. Sounds a bit perfect right? How is this possible for any woman, let alone a working mom to accomplish all this? Many look at the Proverbs 31 woman as accomplishing all that she had all at the same time. That she was nursing her children while juggling these responsibilities. But have you ever looked at her accomplishments, as her *life's accomplishments*? Have you ever thought she was once single, childless, and even retired? The Proverbs 31 woman accomplished her purpose over the course of her life.

So what season of life are you currently in? How has God called you to serve in this season of life? God wants us to serve Him with wisdom in light of our current season. Singles are able to serve God with freedom and flexibility. Married women without children can explore their new ministry with their husbands. Mothers with children in the home can serve God by ministering to her husband and children. And older women can pour into the younger, passing on wisdom to the next generation.

Reign in the Now

What has God called you to do right now? How do your passions, talents, and spiritual gifts direct your "right now" call? Your unique experiences and desires will also guide you to your *individual* and *right now* calls.

Looking Back

1. What *unique experiences* have you encountered? How can these experiences be used to encourage others?

2. What areas of service do you feel most passionate about? (Children, women, families, elderly, disabled persons, homeless etc.) How do you see God calling you to serve in these areas?

3. List your natural talents (singing, writing, athletics, artistry, numbers etc.)

4. List your spiritual gifts.

My Design
T + P+ G= My Design

My Talents_____

My Passions_____

My Spiritual Gifts_____

1. Your talents, passions, and spiritual gifts are not by chance? It's God's divine design specifically for you. How do you see your T+P+G supporting each other?

2. With your "design" in mind, how would you describe your individual call and "right now" call?

Confirming Your Call

Plans fail for lack of counsel, but with many advisers they succeed (Proverbs 15:22 NIV).

It is important to confirm your call and spiritual gifts. We are most effective when we serve in the right place, so we need others to help us get to the right place. We must put our gifts into action to determine if we are indeed called to these areas. Do you enjoy it? Do others respond well to you? Should you invest time to further develop that gift? Next, other believers can confirm your calling. Others will see your growth and effectiveness in a certain area, and will confirm your gifting. Finally, be open to the wisdom of others and ask your pastors or mentors to help you identify your gifts.

Spiritual Discipline in Action

"Faith comes from hearing, and they are going to hear it from me!" said Angela. Angela recognized her gift to clearly explain the gospel of Christ and lead others to accept Christ as their Savior. Others affirmed her gift of evangelism, and she began to help equip others to share the gospel of Christ. Angela took honor in knowing God had empowered her to help save the lost. Her rule for life was to "talk to everyone about Jesus!" The spiritual discipline of *rule for life* is a motto that helps to guide and focus our living. Let's look at how we can focus and commit to utilizing our spiritual gifts.

Discipline—*Rule for Life*

Purpose: Create a motto for life that helps guide and keep our lives focused. Rules for life help us move towards what we want in life, while also reminding us of God's truth.

Spend 20 min in prayer to consider a "rule for life" in this current season. Ask God to lead you to words and actions that will motivate you to commit to your purpose.

Consider these questions:
1. What spiritual disciplines do you enjoy the most?
2. How do you enjoy connecting with God? (Journaling, prayer, worship etc.)
3. What areas in your life would you like to improve?
4. Where do we find our identity or self-worth?

Sample *Rules for Life*

- I will find my worth in Christ, and in Christ alone
- God has given me gifts and talents, I will make the most of my gifts
- I will talk to someone about Jesus everyday
- I will live to Reflect God

My Rule for Life:

_____

_____

_____

_____

Chapter Overview

1. You are so special to God and vital to the body of Christ. No one else can do what you were called to do.

2. Throughout the Bible, women have contributed to the work of God.

3. Romans Chapter 16 means so much to a woman discovering her ministry and place in the body of Christ. Out of a list 27 names in chapter 16, 10 are women. Paul not only lists their names, but also praises them for their ministry.

4. The call on your life can be divided into three categories—*General* Call, *Individual* Call and, the "*Right Now*" Call.

5. The "Proverbs 31 Woman" is a great example of a *life of service*. Many become overwhelmed at the thought of her capability and accomplishments to the point of deeming her unattainable and not a real woman.

6. The Proverbs 31 woman accomplished her purpose over the course of her life. You too are called to a life of service.

7. Your unique experiences and desires will also guide you to your individual and right now calls.

8. It is important to confirm your call and spiritual gifts because we are most effective when we serve in the right place.

Related Scriptures

- 1 Peter 4:10-11
- John 12:26
- Romans 12:10-11
- Colossians 3:23-24

CHAPTER 12

Reign in Your Worth

But God shows his love for us in that while
we were still sinners, Christ died for us
(Romans 5:8 ESV).

Worth means value, significance, or importance. You are significant to God! So significant, He desires to share His image and likeness with you. So valuable, He sent His only Son to redeem you. So important, He will use your life to save the lives of others. God thinks so highly of you and you are a treasure in His eyes. Will you see yourself the way your heavenly Father sees you? Will you commit to living the life God has created you to live?

God has already empowered you and He has already paid the price for you to live in your worth. Every chapter of this book was written in an effort to help you see yourself through the lenses of our Creator. It's all in an effort to help you understand: What God thinks about you should matter most! Our self-esteem and how others view us should pale in comparison to God's divine and perfect view of you. God says you are awesome, and that settles it!

God Sees Us Through Jesus

There are many photo filters that change and enhance photos. But, there's no greater filter than the one God sees us through—Jesus! When God looks at us, He sees what His Son did on the cross. When God looks at us, He sees our true identity. For example, instead of seeing sinners, He sees the redeemed. Instead of seeing guilt and shame, He sees a testimony that will save lives. Isn't it amazing how God can look past our sin and brokenness to see the best in us? Isn't it amazing how God allows the perfection of Christ to be credited to us?

That was God's plan all along: to send His Son to die, so He could view us this way. So we too, could view ourselves through the lens of Christ. This lens refocuses our eyes on God's predestined plan for our lives. As we refocus and correct our vision, we see the truth in how we were created. We learned how we were created lends to our value and purpose. These corrective lenses reveal how we were created to *reflect*, *relate*, and *reign*. This renewed vision of ourselves is the first step in living the life God created you to live.

Reign in Excellence

By his divine power, God has given us everything we need for living a godly life. We have received all of this by coming to know him, the one who called us to himself by means of his marvelous glory and excellence (2 Peter 1:3 NLT).

God has given us all we need to live a godly life. God has also given us all we need to live the life He has called us to live. Peter explains how we are equipped for godly living by coming to know the creator and savior of the world. God has called us to Himself, not only to have a relationship with us, but also to call us into His glory and excellence.

Think about it. What does it mean to be called into God's excellence? To be called into His glory? It means the Creator of all things has called you into His spotlight. It's like God won an Academy Award but instead of accepting the award; He calls you up on stage. He did the work, but He shares His glory with us. He calls you on stage to let the world see you for who you really are, and applaud you. What an amazing God we serve? Well . . . actually, what an amazing God who serves us! All other religions and faiths are rooted in what you can do for God. But, the Christian faith is all about what God does for us. All we have to do is believe and live in our calling. The excellence God has called you to is your unique calling. God desires to shine the spotlight on you; will you step into the light?

The Acceptance Speech

God has just called you on stage. Take a few moments and think through how you would address the crowd. What is God calling you to do?

Step Into the Light

You are the light of the world. A town built on a hill cannot be hidden. Neither do people light a lamp and put it under a bowl. Instead they put it on its stand, and it gives light to everyone in the house. In the same way, let your light shine before others, that they may see your good deeds and glorify your Father in heaven (Matthew 5:14-16).

It's time to step into the light. God calls us a city on a hill and a light to the world. Being light to the world means we put our identity in Christ into action. You have learned the facts of who you are in Christ, now it's about acts. Actions, works, and fruit all display the transforming work of the Spirit within us. Now that we know better, we do better. We no longer allow a false identity or a lack of self-worth to dictate our actions and hold us captive. We have freedom to live in our calling.

As God shines His light on you, are you willing to step into the light? Are you ready to be an example and force of change in your community, church, family, workplace, or school? There is no denying that God is calling you. The question is: will you respond with a yes?

Mirror, Mirror, on the Wall

What do you see? Do you see a woman of value and significance? Do you see an ambassador for Christ with a unique purpose and story to tell? The journey has been called beyond the mirror, seeing yourself the way God sees you. Can you finally see yourself through the eyes of Christ? The book of James gives an illustration of a person who disobeys the commands of Christ. He says the one who hears the Word of God and disobeys it, is like a man who looks in the mirror and instantly forgets what he looks like (James 1). I believe when we live outside of our calling, or allow sin and fear to keep us in bondage; it's because we have forgotten our identity in Christ. We forget what God sees, so we operate in what we see.

Thy Kingdom Come

Do you remember the Lord's Prayer? *Thy kingdom come, Thy will be done in earth, as it is in heaven* is the Lord's desire for you to live the life you were created to live. It's a prayer for us to live out the will of God on earth. To live it out, amongst the hurting people around us. To live it out amongst the people who have hurt us. To live it out and bring light to a dark world. The light God shines upon you and the excellence He shares with you is not for you. It's for your loved ones, co-workers, classmates, and even your enemies.

I pray this journey helps you take hold of the great inheritance we have as Image Bearers. That you continue this journey of transforming your spiritual eyes to see what God sees; that you live out your purpose and reign in your calling.

Spiritual Discipline in Action

Celebrate God all day, every day. I mean, revel in him!
(Philippians 4:4 MSG).

My first collegiate softball practice was nearly complete. I was exhausted from the fast pace of practice and the pressure to make a good first impression. Just when I thought practice was over, coach called us together for one final drill. He explained the drill, "We need to get three final outs, then we celebrate! Since our goal is to win a National Championship . . . we need to practice celebrating our future victory!"

This was literally the best part of practice. There was no pressure to be perfect or prove my ability. All I needed to do was throw my glove down, and have fun celebrating. Not only celebrate what has already happened, but celebrate what is to come!

Can you imagine living a life expecting to win? A life where we celebrate the future victories God has in store for us? The Bible encourages the church not to be worried or anxious for anything, but instead rejoice and pray with thanksgiving! It teaches us how a focus on thanksgiving and rejoicing leads to peace.

God loves when we celebrate. He loves when we trust and place our hope in Him to win on our behalf. He loves when our celebration for future victories leads to peace and rest. Just like the best part of practice was the celebration; the best parts of our lives can be when we practice (or create a habit) to celebrate and thank God before He acts! The spiritual discipline of *celebration* allows us to find peace and rest in the joyful celebration of our amazing God.

Discipline—*Celebration*
Purpose: To take joy and pleasure in God, to move the spirit towards praise, worship, and gratitude.

Spend 20 min in prayer praying about the victories you have encountered while on this journey, and list them. Thank God and praise Him for the many victories He has won on your behalf. Thank God for the future victories He will continue to have on your behalf.

Celebration DANCE—Now get up and have a good ol' dance for the Lord. Have fun, and just do it!

Appendix A:

Spiritual Gifts Survey

Directions: The 84 statements below will help to guide you to your spiritual gifts. Respond to each statement below according to how each statement best represents yourself. Answer each question honestly as there are no right or wrong answers. Do your best to respond with your first initial thought. This survey, although not definite, will help lead you to where God has designed you to serve.

Response Choices:
5- Always / definitely true for me
4- Most of the time/ true for me
3- Half of the time/true about me
2- Occasionally/ true about me
1- Rarely/ True about me
0- Never/ True about me

Spiritual Gift Statement	Response
1. I am capable of communicating vision and goals clearly.	
2. I easily see precise steps to accomplish a goal.	
3. I enjoy teaching others about the Bible.	
4. I desire for others to go deeper in their relationship with God.	
5. I have a strong desire to speak God's truth, even on difficult topics.	
6. I desire to see Christian ministry take place outside of the church.	
7. I have been successful in helping others accept Christ as their Savior.	
8. I naturally encourage others.	
9. I have the ability to sense the motives of people.	
10. I think to trust God first in difficult situations.	
11. I am a person that takes action.	
12. When I meet new people at church, I have a desire to make them feel welcomed.	
13. I hurt when others around me hurt.	
14. I do not have a hard time tithing and financially supporting to ministry needs.	
15. I am able to rally others to commit to accomplishing ministry goals.	
16. I pay attention to details.	
17. I am able to provide practical examples to explain Biblical truths.	
18. I am protective of others and care for their spiritual wellbeing.	
19. Often times I feel I have a message from God to share.	

Spiritual Gift Statement	Response
20. God has given me vision to start a new ministry to serve the underserved.	
21. I enjoy speaking to strangers about Jesus.	
22. I have the ability to challenge others to live for God.	
23. I can sense if someone is being honest or authentic.	
24. Romans 8:28 "all things work for the good" is my life verse.	
25. I do not mind working behind the scenes to help accomplish goals.	
26. I have the ability of making others feel welcomed.	
27. I am sensitive to the struggles of others and want to help them.	
28. I love meeting the needs of others by giving of my financial resources.	
29. I enjoy being the "point person" on projects.	
30. In a group setting, I can see how everyone can contribute and will delegate tasks.	
31. I have a desire to study the Bible more deeply than others.	
32. I have been successful in helping others grow in their faith.	
33. On occasions God has given me a word or message to share with an individual or group; and have felt compelled to share it.	
34. I can see myself being on a team that starts a new church.	
35. I have a strong desire for everyone to accept Jesus as their Savior.	
36. I motivate others to put their faith into action.	
37. I can quickly determine if a statement is Biblical.	

Spiritual Gift Statement	Response
38. I trust God will answer all prayers according to His will.	
39. I serve others by completing practical needs for them.	
40. I enjoy hosting others at my home.	
41. People feel comfortable talking about their hurts with me.	
42. I am generous with my time and other resources.	
43. I use my influence to move others towards their God given purpose.	
44. I enjoy organizing and doing things in an orderly fashion.	
45. I can simplify and explain the Bible to new or non- believers.	
46. I am willing to take the initiative in helping others grow in their faith.	
47. Others have recognized that God has spoken a word directly to them through my message.	
48. I enjoy traveling to new places to share about Christ.	
49. I have the ability to explain salvation and how to receive it.	
50. I tend to see potential in others and feel compelled to tell them.	
51. When people share about their faith, I tend to listen carefully to determine if they are speaking the truth about Christ.	
52. I trust God even when everything seems to go wrong.	
53. I see the needs of people and I step in to help.	
54. I serve others by cooking for them.	
55. People have thanked me for helping them in low points of their lives.	

Spiritual Gift Statement	Response
56. I encourage others to give of their resources to support Christian ministry.	
57. I am willing to take risks to grow the body of Christ.	
58. I am successful at creating action plans for projects or events.	
59. I am willing to study and prepare to teach the Bible regularly.	
60. I prayer for others.	
61. I am sensitive to God's truth: what's right and what's wrong or what's just and unjust.	
62. I want to bring the Gospel of Christ to those who do not go to church.	
63. I can clearly explain the Gospel of Christ.	
64. I enjoy the opportunity to counsel or comfort others in need.	
65. I can determine if a statement is true about Jesus.	
66. I influence others to stay faithful and trust God when things are difficult.	
67. I'm energized by getting things done.	
68. When I see outsiders, I'm intentional to meet and get to know them.	
69. I have hope for those who others have given up on.	
70. I am a generous giver.	
71. I see big picture rather than small details.	
72. I believe all ministries, events, and project should be well planned and staffed properly in order to be successful.	
73. I get energized after teaching about God.	
74. I feel a strong desire and passion to minister to others.	

Spiritual Gift Statement	Response
75. I have felt compelled to share advice, warnings, and even instruction to others.	
76. I have been successful in starting new ministries.	
77. I feel comfortable talking to people of other faiths about Jesus.	
78. I'm comfortable approaching and encouraging those who have stumbled in their faith.	
79. Others have told me I have a good judgment of character.	
80. I believe God will get glory in every situation.	
81. I enjoy completing everyday task to support the church.	
82. My home tends to be the place others chose to gather.	
83. I have compassion for people in tough times.	
84. I believe God has blessed me to be a blessing to others.	

Appendix A Cont.:

Scoring Your Survey

Scoring Your Survey

Directions: Place your score (0-5) in the box corresponding to the statement. Next, add your responses for each spiritual gift, place your total score in the final box. Finally circle your 3 highest scores.

Leadership	1	15	29	43	57	71	=
Administration	2	16	30	44	58	72	=
Teaching	3	17	31	45	59	73	=
Pastor	4	18	32	46	60	74	=
Prophecy	5	19	33	47	61	75	=
Apostleship	6	20	34	48	62	76	=
Evangelism	7	21	35	49	63	77	=
Encouragement	8	22	36	50	64	78	=
Discernment	9	23	37	51	65	79	=
Faith	10	24	38	52	66	80	=
Service/Helps	11	25	39	53	67	81	=
Hospitality	12	26	40	54	68	82	=

| Mercy | 13 | 27 | 41 | 55 | 69 | 83 | = |
| Giving | 14 | 28 | 42 | 56 | 70 | 84 | = |

What were the 3 highest scoring gifts from the survey?

1. _____
2. _____
3. _____

Response to the Survey

1. Do you agree or disagree with the results of the survey?

2. Did any of the results surprise you? If so, how?

3. How can these gifts support your natural talents and passions?

4. How do you see God using these gifts in your unique service/ministry to the Body of Christ?

Appendix B:

Small Group Guide

*B*eyond the Mirror is a discipleship resource designed to help women find their true identity and worth in Christ. The goal of *Beyond the Mirror* is to teach biblical truths of how and why we were created, in order to steer women in the direction of their true purpose and calling. *Beyond the Mirror* answers the question of "Why am I here?" by exploring how we are created to *relate, reflect,* and *reign.*

This guide is designed to take a group of women through a 10-week study. It serves as a guide for discussion of chapter content, prompts for experiential exercises, and a springboard for feedback. Each weekly discussion consists of: (1) *Warm-up,* which can serve as a fun study Ice Breaker. (2) *Chapter Recap* serves as prompts to guide chapter overview. (3) *Reflection Questions,* which lend to deeper spiritual discovery. (4) *Spiritual Discipline in Action* gives feedback and debrief of personal experience with the spiritual discipline exercise.

Small group leaders are welcomed to use this guide as an outline to create their own study. Feel free to add your own creative ideas, and customize this study for your women. Chapter recap questions are stated below:

Chapter Recap: (10 min)

Take about 10 min to discuss what stood out from the reading. Here are a few questions to consider:

1. How did the reading specially speak to you?
2. What new insights did you learn about your creation story?
3. How did the reading challenge you (to change your thinking or actions)?

Week 1—Your Creation Story

Read: Introduction and Chapter 1
Warm- up: Mirror; Mirror (5-10 min)

Share your experience with the "Mirror Mirror" activity. As you were asked to write down "what do you see?" what initial emotions and thoughts came to the surface? Were you able to write down your honest thoughts about yourself? How may what your personal thoughts differ from how others see you (personal opinions vs. the opinion of others)?

Chapter Recap: (10 min)
Chapter Reflection: (10-15min)

1. What about David's selection as king stands out to you? How does this biblical example personally speak to you?

2. As God created the heavens and the earth, He created with a "progression of artistry." We are God's masterpiece, created to display His beauty to the world.

How does the truth of how we were created differ from our societal standards of beauty? How is the truth of how God sees us continually replaced with the lies of the world?

3. God didn't create Eve until Adam realized a need for her. Adam knew Eve's true worth. Adam needed Eve. The world also needs you. The next chapter addresses "why we were created"; take a few moments to share with the group why you believe God specially created you?

Spiritual Discipline in Action: (10 min)
Share your experiences of *praying scripture*. Later, take a few moments to look through the Bible and make a list of other Scriptures the group can insert into their prayers. Think of unique situations or seasons of life within the group and add Scriptures, which encourage and speak truth to these situations.

Week 2—Why You Were Created

Read: Chapter 2
Warm- up: Great Inheritance (5-10 min)

Can you imagine receiving an unexpected inheritance; an inheritance that made you an heir to fortunes? What would you buy first? How would you use this power? Share with the group what you would honestly do with a great financial inheritance.

Now, think of the inheritance we have received from our heavenly Father. As we are entrusted to bear the Image of

God, how may the list above (how you would spend your financial inheritance) differ from how we put our spiritual inheritance to use? Why?

Chapter Recap: (10 min)
Chapter Reflection: (10-15min)

1. You were created to be an heir, to handle the business of your heavenly Father. Does this responsibility inspire you or frighten you? And why?

2. In the Old Testament Scripture, the word *blessing* is *bārak (baw-rak')* that means, kneel; bless; to bestow power for success. How has the reading helped you to believe God has blessed you to succeed in His plan for your life?

3. List the ways God provided for Mary, the mother of Jesus (Hint: physical protection, companionship, etc.). Which provision helps you believe that God will also provide for you?

4. Mary was a teenager facing social humiliation, but was willing to give herself wholly to the will of God. Mary was willing to trust God even when she didn't have all of the answers. What might be holding you back from giving yourself wholly to the will of God?

Spiritual Discipline in Action: (10 min)
Share your experiences of the *Bible Study* discipline. What does God's response to Mary, Jeremiah, and Moses reveal about His character? How can you apply God's response to your own life?

172 • BEYOND THE MIRROR

Week 3—Created to Relate

Read: Chapter 3
Warm- up: Our Basic Needs (5-10 min)

Write a list of what you need to survive. Be specific and share your list with the group. Are there any differences or similarities?

Maslow's hierarchy of needs is a theory in psychology proposed by Abraham Maslow. Maslow explains the basic human needs are physiological (air, water, and food), safety (physical, financial, health) belongingness/love (relationships, family, and intimacy), esteem (self -respect), self-actualization (becoming all you can be), and self-transcendence (spirituality or belief in a high power). What is most important to you? What you think is most important to God?

Now think of the inheritance we have received from our heavenly Father. As we are entrusted to bear the Image of God, how may the list above (how you would spend your financial inheritance) differ from how we put our spiritual inheritance to use? Why?

Chapter Recap: (10 min)
Chapter Reflection: (10-15min)

1. If everyone viewed themselves and others as "Image Bearers," how differently do you think we would treat each other?

2. Knowing unity in relationships brings honor to God, how will you strive to bring unity in your relationships? What may be barriers or difficulties in mending some relationships in your life?

4. God desires to be a part of every aspect of our lives. What life decisions have you made independent of God? What were the results of those decisions? What steps can you take to begin including God in your decision-making?

Spiritual Discipline in Action: (10 min)
Share your experiences of the *Self-Examination and Confession* discipline. How did the Scripture reference inform you of sin in your own life? Discuss and share the possible roots of the sin present in your life. Pray with and for each other, pray for victory over these areas of sin.

Week 4—Created to Reflect

Read: Chapter 4
Warm- up: Breaking a Mirror (5-10 min)

Have you ever heard of the superstition of breaking a mirror? The one where you are doomed with seven years of bad luck! Do you have any clue why this myth equates breaking a mirror to seven years of bad luck?

(Hopefully no one read ahead) But, the myth believes the mirror not only reflects the physical, but the soul of the person. The damaged mirror now reflects the damaged soul of the one who broke the mirror, so, why seven years? Legends believe it's rooted in the Roman belief that every seven year we are renewed or get a second chance in life.

Whether you believe in superstitions or not, the broken mirror analogy relates to our brokenness before God. We were created to reflect the Image of God, however, sin affects our ability to reflect God fully. As broken mirrors, we reflect remnants of God, but the good news is: we don't have to wait seven years to renew the image we reflect. It can start today!

Chapter Recap: (10 min)
Chapter Reflection: (10-15min)

1. What does it mean to reflect the image of God?

2. What damages our reflection of God? What in your personal relationship may restrict you from reflecting God fully?

3. Since we do not have to wait every seven years to get right with God, what did God do to help us restore our reflection of Him?

4. The Bible teaches that Jesus Christ was the God-man, fully God and fully human. Why did God's once-and-for-all sacrifice need to be fully human and fully God?

5. How would you describe salvation? What is our role in salvation (hint: faith in Jesus)? How does the "once-and-for-all sacrifice" of God stand against the myth of the seven year (broken mirror example) renewal?

Spiritual Discipline in Action: (10 min)
Share your experiences of the *Prayer of Recollection* discipline. Discuss where you stand in the "new self" vs. "old self" conversation. Discuss any difficulties you may have in claiming the "old" as old and the "new" as new.

Week 5—Created to Reign

Read: Chapter 5
Warm- up: What do you mean reign? (5-10 min)

Read this Scripture to the Group: *This saying is trustworthy: For if we have died with Him, we will also live with Him; if we endure, we will also reign with Him* (2 Timothy 2:11-12a HCSB).

Discuss the verse in chunks (the saying is trustworthy; stop and discuss). Ask the group what feelings or questions come to mind. Finally discuss what thoughts or feelings come to mind when we think of ourselves as one who was created to "reign." Does this create conflict or does it encourage you as a woman? Explain why. Keep this in mind as you recap the chapter.

Chapter Recap: (10 min)
Chapter Reflection: (10-15min)

1. Paul calls us a "royal priesthood," which means we are a body of kingly priests with access to God through Christ. What do you believe this means for believers in general, and what does this mean for you?

2. Before the resurrection of Christ, God's people could not confess their sin or receive forgiveness without a priest. However, Christ changed all of this. Christ is now our High Priest and serves as our mediator to the Father. Because of Christ we can now approach God and share intimacy with Him. How does this help you to understand your role as a "royal priesthood?"

3. In the same breath, Paul calls us a royal priesthood, a chosen people, and a special possession. How do these labels help you to see yourself from God's point of view?

4. You are a "royal priesthood" chosen to declare the glory of God. How do you feel about adding the title of priest or minister to your name? Would you ever consider yourself a minister? What do you believe your roles or duties as a priest would be?

5. God desires that we reign, that we live an abundant life, and that we live in His purpose for our lives. Many are misled to believe they are reigning in life (like Paul). Have you ever been misled to believe you reigned, but were actually outside of the will of God? If so, explain.

Spiritual Discipline in Action: (10 min)
Share your experiences of the *Detachment* discipline. Discuss the following questions:

1. Paul relied heavily on his heritage, citizenship, and education as a source of pride and identity. List any labels or successes you may currently associate with as a source of pride.

2. How would you describe yourself without the above labels? Take a few minutes to describe yourself without using any of the above labels and without listing any of your accomplishments.

3. How has your self-worth been associated with success and labels?

Week 6—Reign as a Disciple

Read: Chapter 6
Warm- up: Are you Dusty? (5-10 min)

Take this warm-up time to discuss these two questions:

1. How does the "Dust" explanation of discipleship
   change your perception on what it means to be a
   Christian?

2. What does the "Dust" explanation show you about
   the character of God?

3. All of us owe our salvation (to Christ alone, however)
   to those who continue to spread the good news of
   Christ. Let's take a moment to pray and thank God
   for those who have shared Christ with us.

Chapter Recap: (10 min)
Chapter Reflection: (10-15min)

1. In Christ, we have a teacher that not only wants us to
   actively grow and mature as students, but also grow
   as a friend. Share your feelings of viewing Christ as
   a teacher, and as a friend.

2. If prayer leads to a relationship with God, how often
   should we pray? What can you do to increase and improve our prayer routine?

3. James 5:16 says, *The prayers of the righteous are
   powerful and effective.* What makes prayer "powerful

and effective"? How can we become more effective in our prayers?

4. The Bible helps to reveal the character and voice of God. What have you learned that gives you more confidence in the Bible?

Spiritual Discipline in Action: (10 min)
Share your experiences of the *praying Scripture* discipline. Discuss the following question: Do you have any difficulties believing God has truly forgiven you? Please share why and in what situations is it hard to accept God's forgiveness.

Use Romans 8:31-37 as your closing prayer.

Week 7—Reign in Obedience and Faith

Read: Chapter 7 & 8
Warm- up: Faith to Obey (5-10 min)

When we repent (turning from sin towards God), we must have faith in what we are turning to. Turning away from sin and turning to Christ would actually lead to living in our purpose and leading an abundant life. When we repent, we aren't merely turning away from sin; but turning to something greater!

In your journals, draw a vertical line down the middle of a page. On one side write "The Cost of Discipleship," on the other write "The Cost of Non-Discipleship." As a group fill in both sides.

Chapter Recap: (10 min)

Chapter Reflection: (10-15min)

1. What is the difference between obedience and Lordship? It is possible one may appear to be obedient to God, yet not live under His lordship? Explain and give examples.

2. The story of the rich Young Ruler challenges us to submit our all to Christ. If Jesus was to tell you: "You lack one thing," what would that one thing be?

3. Think of the story of Zacchaeus, think of his heart vs. what others thought of him. How does this story challenge you? (Passing judgment, the heart vs. actions)

4. What does the obedience of Christ and His suffering teach you about His character and love?

5. Faith pleases God. Take time to talk through the *Parable of the Sower*. Describe the soils and give real life examples that could be present in our lives.

6. What can we learn from the women who touched Jesus?

Spiritual Discipline in Action: (10 min)
Share your experiences of the *Witness* discipline. Partner up and share your quick (3min) testimony with each other.

Week 8—Reign in Your Purpose

Read: Chapter 9
Warm- up: For Such a Time as This (5-10 min)

Esther and the Samaritan Woman had a unique task to fulfill. Their courage to speak up saved the physical and spiritual lives of others. Share a moment where you or a woman you know spoke up for others. How do these testimonies encourage you to be willing to share your story?

Chapter Recap: (10 min)
Chapter Reflection: (10-15min)

1. *We are citizens of heaven, where the Lord Jesus Christ lives. And we are eagerly waiting for him to return as our Savior* (Philippians 3:20 NLT). Paul reminds us that we are citizens of Heaven, and we are Ambassadors for Christ. What does the title of Ambassador reveal about your purpose?

2. Where has God currently placed you to represent Him as an Ambassador? And, what do you believe God has called you to specifically do in these places?

3. What unique experiences have you encountered? How can these experiences be used to encourage others?

4. What areas of service do you feel most passionate about? (Children, women, families, elderly, disabled persons, etc.) How do you see God calling you to serve in these areas?

5. If you were to dream and create a job description including both your unique experiences and passion to serve; what would it look like? (Create a name for the position, and then write your duties and responsibilities.

Spiritual Discipline in Action: (10 min)
Share your experiences of *sharing your desires with God* discipline. Where you able to be honest and vulnerable with God? Did you hold back? Where there any fears? Fear of judgment, or fear that your desires are not what God has in store for you?

Week 9—Reign in the Body of Christ

Read: Chapter 10
Warm- up: You've got Talent (5-10 min)

Do you have a unique, random, or wacky talent? Take this time to let loose and share your wacky talents with each other.

Chapter Recap: (10 min)
Chapter Reflection: (10-15min)

1. As an official or unofficial title, God empowers us to serve in Christian ministry. Do you feel comfortable with the title of minister? What may be your reservations? What excites you about this title?

2. Before reading this chapter, what was your perception of your own spiritual gifts? Did any of the spiritual gift definitions change your perception of ministry?

Spiritual Discipline in Action: (10 min)
Share your experiences of the *Pray, Study, and Survey* discipline. What did you discover? What excites you? How can we affirm and confirm these gifts in each other?

Week 10—Reign Through Serving in Your Worth

Read: Chapter 11 & 12
Warm- up: Acceptance Speech (5-10 min)

God has called you into the spotlight and on to the stage. Share your acceptance speech with the group.

Chapter Recap: (10 min)
Chapter Reflection: (10-15min)

1. Women in Ministry can sometime be a touchy subject. Wherever you stand on this subject, what has Romans 16 shown you about the vital influence of women serving in their gifts?

2. What *unique experiences* have you encountered? How can these experiences be used to encourage others?

3. What areas of service do you feel most *passionate about*? (Children, women, families, elderly, disabled persons, homeless etc.) How do you see God calling you to serve in these areas?

SMALL GROUP GUIDE • 183

4. Share your "My Design" results. Your talents, passions, and spiritual gifts are not by chance? It's God's divine design specifically for you. How do you see your T+P+G supporting each other?

5. With your "design" in mind, how would you describe your individual call and "right now" call?

6. The Proverbs 31 Women is about a life of service. How does this perspective of the Proverbs 31 woman help you view your "call"?

Spiritual Discipline in Action: (10 min)

Share your experiences of the *Rule for Life* discipline. Share your "Rule for Life" with each other. Take this time to pray for the courage to live this rule out in your life. Celebrate all God has revealed, changed, and motivated you to do while on this journey.

Notes

[1] Willard, Dallas, *Renovation of the Heart: Putting On the Character of Christ*. NavPress, 2012.

[2] Kidner, Derek. *Genesis*. Edited by DJ Wiseman. Downers Grove: Intervarsity Press, 1967. 60.

[3] Benson, Joseph. "St. John." *The New Testament of Our Lord and Savior Jesus Christ*. Vol. 1. New York: Carlton & Phillips, 1854. 646

[4] Holoman, Henry. "Fall." *Kregel Dictionary of the Bible and Theology*. Grand Rapids: Kregel Publications, 2005. 141

[5] Benner, David G., *Care of Souls*. Grand Rapids: Baker Books, 1998. 95

[6] Holoman, Henry. "Image of God." *Kregel Dictionary of the Bible and Theology*. Grand Rapids: Kregel Publications, 2005. 226.

[7] Holoman, Henry. "Bible." *Kregel Dictionary of the Bible and Theology*. Grand Rapids: Kregel Publications, 2005. 51

About the Author

Ta'Tyana Leonard is a licensed minister who serves at Mission Eben Ezer Family Church of Carson, CA. Ta'Tyana also serves as Director of Ministries for Fellowship of Christian Athletes (FCA) of Los Angeles. Ta'Tyana received a Master's Degree in Women's Ministry from Talbot School of Theology, and her heart's passion is to help women live in their true worth and purpose.

Born and raised in Los Angeles, Ta'Tyana Leonard has found ways to succeed by the grace of God and the support of both her natural and spiritual families. As a member of Sunnyside Baptist Church she discovered her love for God and singing. While Attending Washington Preparatory High School, Ta'Tyana graduated with academic and athletic honors. Ta'Tyana continues to hold the Los Angeles City Strikeout record of 1,086, and after being honored as Major League Baseball's Charity-RBI Player of the Year for three consecutive years; had her number (#1) retired for her success on and off the field. After graduating from Washington Prep, Ta'Tyana continued on to Oregon State University on a full softball Scholarship.

At Oregon State University Ta'Tyana made history by becoming the first African American Pitcher at OSU and only the second in the Pac-10 Conference, helping to lead OSU to their first NCAA World Series appearance. Upon graduating with a BS in Business Administration from Oregon State University; Ta'Tyana took on many leadership roles on campus as Student Athlete Advisory Committee (SAAC) volunteer coordinator and Female Champions for Christ Campus Ministry Leader. Garnishing awards as All Region Academic Team, 1st All Pac-10 Academic Team Honors, Arthur Ash Diversity and Leadership Award Winner,

186 • BEYOND THE MIRROR

and a Lowe's Senior of the Year Nominee. Ta'Tyana also traveled Europe playing professionally in The Netherlands for the Haarlem Terrasvogels; winning the 2008 Dutch National Championship. Ta'Tyana used every opportunity to minister to her teammates and is a true "Champion for Christ!"

While serving with FCA as a campus minister to South LA public high schools, Ta'Tyana recognized the dark reality of sin. The dark reality left mere teenagers to live in the brokenness of depression, promiscuity, sex trade, homosexuality, and abortion. At such a young age these women were carrying heavy loads of shame and guilt. Ta'Tyana needed arsenal to combat the harsh reality of sin's stain on her community; so she started to write. She developed resources to help point these women to Christ, instead of pointing to their sin.

After becoming a "big sister" to these girls, Ta'Tyana identified the common root of their brokenness. self- worth! These young women did not know their true worth and settled for discounts. How we view ourselves is so important because it will affect our decision making, how we see others, and ultimately determines our success in life. God wants us to seek our true worth in Him, not in the standards of the world. *Beyond the Mirror* will help lead women to their true identity and purpose in Christ.

Acknowledgements

I would like to thank my husband Adam for supporting me and this book writing journey. Thank you for putting up with my late nights and my cranky mornings. I love you and pray you are proud of the finish product! I would also like to thank my family and church families (Mission Eben Ezer and Sunnyside Baptist Church) for all of your support and encouragement.

Thank you to my Fellowship of Christian Athletes family for also supporting this journey. Thank you for the opportunity to serve alongside you in ministry. I would also like to thank Tommy Draffen, Kevin Nickerson, Bill Beazley, George Hicker, Josh Canales, Evan Money, and Mike Keaton for all of your support of the FCA ministry. These seven years on staff have bred life within me; and I know we have left an eternal impact on the Kingdom of God.

I would like to thank my sisters in Christ for all of your support. Thank you Tuccoa Polk and Bethany Wilkes for your input and revisions. I could not have done this without you. Thank you Dianne Sargent for your final editing services and encouragement.

Finally I would like to thank Isaiah Bouie (Photography), Charlotte Vincent (Dress Design), and Brianne Smith (Hair and Make-up) for their contributions to the overall book design.

#MIRRORJOURNEY

Join the Conversation

- Register your small group or book club
- Sign up for group discussion material
- Subscribe to latest blog posts and devotionals

Stay Connected Follow: @tatyana_leonard

WWW. TATYANALEONARD. COM

Photography: Isaiah Bouie
Dress Designer: Charlotte Vincent
Hair and Make-up: Breann Smith